Wow! This is t
Revival is like v
Jesus and two of his twenty-first century disciples—Ed Hird and David Kitz. Share their excitement as Jesus opens their minds to the Old Testament prophecies about Himself. With the added benefit of New Testament insights and lessons from history, we see the Holy Spirit preparing to ignite fresh revival fires in our day.

—Don Hutchinson
Pastor, lawyer, and author of *Church in Society: First Century Citizenship Lessons for Twenty-First Century Christians*

My initial reaction to drawing a parallel between two "dynamic duos"—Elijah/Elisha and John the Baptist/ Jesus—was not favorable. The Bible never makes such a claim. Or so I thought, until I read *The Elisha Code and the Coming Revival*. I did so mainly because co-author Ed Hird is one of my oldest and dearest friends. I was genuinely surprised at the compelling argument he and David Kitz make for this connection as they spur the reader onto revival expectation.

—Alan Gilman
Bible Teacher, Writer, & Podcaster

I found *The Elisha Code and the Coming Revival* by David Kitz & Dr. Ed Hird to be a rollercoaster-thrill-read from beginning to end ... I could not put it down! The authors take you on an adventure of discovery—seeking bold faith—in readiness for the revival to come.

—Alan Kearns
Devotional Treasures blogger, Glenrothes, Scotland

The Elisha Code and the Coming Revival unpacks an intriguing and thought-provoking case for Jesus being the New Testament Elisha, thus carrying out His role as Prophet (along with Priest and King)—not abolishing the Law and the Prophets but fulfilling them. As was needed in the time of both Elisha and Jesus, the book also points us toward spiritual renewal in our increasingly evil world, but with sure and certain hope, and with the promise that, in Jesus, there is true healing and salvation.

—Rev. Laverne Hautz,
Emeritus Lutheran Pastor

If you love God's Word this book is for you! David Kitz and Dr. Hird masterfully connect the Old and New Testaments and brilliantly connect the ministry of Elisha to the ministry we see with Jesus in the Gospels. The thread of practical applications to our own lives is impactful and encouraging. This book is a blueprint for the revival we need in our lives and our churches.

—Andrew Nicholls
Licensed Lay Worship Leader, United Church of Canada

The Elijah Code and the Coming Revival will challenge every believer who has a love for souls and wants to further the kingdom of God. Whether you have been serving God for a couple of years or a lifetime you will be confronted with timeless truths. This book will be a great benefit to many pastors and church leaders.

—Pastor Louie Foster
Durham Foursquare Church

Finally, some common sense! Thank you, David Kitz and Dr. Ed Hird for this timely, Spirit led book. You have managed to cut through the sound of many confusing voices with biblical truth. I believe this book will be a catalyst to see the Elisha Code revealed in this generation with revival fires igniting across the globe!

—Pastor Karen Middleton
Calgary Full Gospel

THE ELISHA CODE

& THE COMING REVIVAL

REDISCOVERING JESUS' BLUEPRINT FOR RENEWAL

DAVID KITZ & DR. ED HIRD

THE ELISHA CODE
Copyright © 2023 by David Kitz & Dr. Ed Hird

Soft cover ISBN: 978-1-4866-2465-2
Hard cover ISBN: 978-1-4866-2466-9
eBook ISBN: 978-1-4866-2467-6

Word Alive Press
119 De Baets Street Winnipeg, MB R2J 3R9
www.wordalivepress.ca

Cataloguing in Publication information can be obtained from Library and Archives Canada.

DEDICATION

This book is dedicated to the memory of our loving parents:

Ewald Kitz
(May 7, 1908—October 27, 1988) and
Wanda Emily (Ziebart) Kitz
(December 28, 1922—July 9, 2022)

and

Edward Victor Hird
(June 17, 1924—June 25, 2019) and
Catherine Lorna Hird
(August 8, 1927—June 9, 2017)

Then I heard a voice from heaven say,
"Write this: Blessed are the dead
who die in the Lord from now on."
"Yes," says the Spirit,
"they will rest from their labor,
for their deeds will follow them."
(Revelation 14:13)

CONTENTS

ACKNOWLEDGEMENTS

We are not blank slates. We are shaped by what we see, hear, read, and experience. So, quite naturally, authors draw on a myriad of ideas and influences that have shaped their beliefs and thinking.

As authors, we both freely acknowledge the crucial role that parents, teachers, and pastors have played in our spiritual and intellectual development. But, specifically, we owe a debt of gratitude to two spiritual giants of the twentieth century.

David Kitz has been deeply influenced by the works of C. S. Lewis. In his writing, Lewis captured the power of symbolism and allegory. He saw below the surface to the deeper meaning of the written text. This quest for a fuller, richer understanding of the Scriptures has led to the book you are now reading.

Similarly, Ed Hird has been profoundly influenced by the missionary evangelist E. Stanley Jones. Jones authored twenty-eight books, and through his life and ministry, he exemplified the hunger for transformative revival which is the underlying theme of this book.

At crucial moments in our writing journey, we were assisted and occasionally corrected by Alan Gilman. His Messianic Jewish perspective added depth to our understanding of the roots of our faith. Alan, we are grateful for your input.

FOREWORD

I became a serious Christian at the tail end of the Jesus movement. I was too young to remember the hippie beads, tie-dyed shirts and "Jesus Is Groovy" slogans, but the songs were still popular when I was in college (including musicians such as Andrae Crouch, Love Song and Second Chapter of Acts), as were the movies—especially *The Cross and the Switchblade*.

The Jesus movement was like a spiritual tsunami that washed over hundreds of thousands of young people in the late 1960s and early '70s and brought them into a personal relationship with Christ. Some of these kids had been drug addicts and social misfits; most were just average Joes and Janes who discovered that Jesus is a lot more exciting than traditional churches had led them to believe.

Lately I find myself waxing nostalgic for those days—not because I want to return to the awkward fashions and hairstyles of 1972, but because I miss the spiritual simplicity of that era. The Jesus movement was primarily focused on—*surprise!*— Jesus. Theology was not complicated, pastors weren't trying to be hip or sophisticated or tech-savvy, and we hadn't yet created a Christian subculture with its own celebrities and political power bases.

Today, we just don't preach enough about Jesus. In today's ultra cool megachurch era, we've become experts on everything but basic Christian theology 101. In my recent travels I've been horrified to learn that many believers have given up the discipline of reading their Bibles even semi-regularly, and very few believers have ever led anyone to faith in Christ. One by one we are trading in our solid moral values for a squishy, spineless, whatever-is-right-for-you faith. People today prefer a steady diet of culturally relevant, fast-paced techno-theology that is a poor substitute for biblical discipleship.

Even many Spirit-filled believers have developed the attitude that a simple focus on Christ isn't enough. We'd rather go to a "prophetic encounter" to hear who will win the next election, or experience some exotic spiritual manifestation (gold dust, gems falling out of the ceiling). Or we prefer to ask Rev. Flash-in-the-Pan to pray for us for the sixteenth time so we can receive yet another "special anointing" that we will probably never use.

In the midst of all this chaos, where is Jesus? Am I the only one out there who is weary of this distraction? Thankfully not. I am so pleased to read this book by Ed Hird and David Kitz because they share my concerns. *The Elisha Code and the Coming Revival* is a refreshing challenge to return to Jesus—and to expect spiritual revival when we clean up our message.

Call me old-fashioned, but I've decided to get back to the basics of the faith. That's why I am reading, *What Jesus Is All About?*, a classic book written 70 years ago by Henrietta Mears, a Bible teacher who helped mentor both Billy Graham and Bill Bright in the 1940s.

Mears explains in her book how each of the four Gospels give us a unique, four-dimensional portrait of the Savior. According to Mears:

- Matthew was written to Jews to tell of a Promised Messiah who is also a King—and it uses the word "kingdom" 55 times.
- Mark was written to Gentiles to tell of a Powerful Savior—and it reports more miracles than any other gospel.
- Luke was written by a Gentile to tell of a Perfect Savior—and it has the most references to Jesus' *humanity.*
- John was written by "the disciple whom Jesus loved" to tell of a Personal Savior—and it has the most references to Jesus' *divine nature.*

The Holy Spirit who inspired the Bible knew we needed more than a one-, two- or three-dimensional look at Jesus. The Spirit gave us a four-dimensional view so that we could gaze at Him from all sides and become captivated by His magnificence—His supreme kingship, His compassionate mercy, His supernatural power, His perfect justice, His amazing humility, and His love for sinners like you and me.

There's so much more to Jesus than we realize. And there is so much more to say about Him than we are telling our generation. Instead of giving people a gospel diluted with left-wing or right-wing politics, or a message mixed with cultural "relevance," we need to give them the real Jesus.

In this insightful book, full of keen insights from the lives of the prophets Elijah and Elisha, the authors challenge us to examine our message, repent of our unfaithfulness and embrace the raw courage to preach Jesus again. As you read this book, please allow God's powerful Word to cut deep.

—J. Lee Grady
Former Editor, *Charisma*
Author, *Follow Me* and *The Holy Spirit Is Not for Sale*
Director, The Mordecai Project

INTRODUCTION

I s there a hidden code to the Bible? Is there some *secret* interpretation—hidden in plain sight—that we have been missing for generations? If so, what is it, and what are the implications for Christians today?

The book you are holding cracks the code—the code Jesus revealed to his disciples. Furthermore, it signals the pattern for the coming global revival, which may well include a host of local revivals marked by miraculous signs and wonders on an unprecedented scale.

We live in dark times—times of fear, pestilence, national and international intrigue, and political turmoil. Many are in despair. But into this darkness, the prophet Isaiah speaks:

> The land of Zebulun and the land of Naphtali,
>> By the way of the sea, beyond the Jordan,
>> Galilee of the Gentiles:
> The people who sat in darkness have seen a great light,
>> And upon those who sat in the region and shadow of death
>> Light has dawned. (Matthew 4:15–16, NKJV)

At the darkest time, in the darkest region, Jesus appeared on the scene. There he began his ministry. In these dark and divided times, as the truth of the Elisha Code is brought to light, we too will see Jesus revealing his grace and power among us.

Throughout the centuries-long history of the church, biblical truths have been lost—lost through sin, unbelief, and neglect—later to be rediscovered by thirsty souls searching for transformative change in dark times. Martin Luther triggered the Reformation with his rediscovery of the truth of salvation by grace through faith. The truth of sanctification triggered the Great Awakening and the Methodist renewal with revival fire-starters such as the Wesley brothers, George Whitefield, and John Newton. The twentieth century began with a fresh outpouring of the Holy Spirit as the truths of Pentecost were brought to the fore through the globe-spanning Welsh revival and the Azusa Street outpouring.

When biblical truth is restored, revival often follows. A harvest of souls is swept into the kingdom of God, as surely as the morning dawns on a new day.

Let's return to God's Holy Word and uncover the foundation Jesus has already laid. Let's return to truths we have overlooked for far too long. Jesus is the Master Builder of the church. By studying his earthly ministry, we can discover the blueprint he was following to launch and establish the church of the first century. It is a blueprint that is patterned after the prophetic Old Testament ministries of Elijah and Elisha.

Within this volume, there are chapters that explore this neglected connection to these two prophets of the old covenant. Often, these chapters are then followed by biographical snapshots of individuals in church history who have tapped into key truths. These principles catapulted the gospel message forward to powerfully impact the world of their time.

To fulfill its divine mission, the church of the twenty-first century does not need to discover new and different truths for this current age. It needs to return to and rediscover lived truths taught by Jesus and the apostles of the first century church, and put into practice by leading men and women of God down through the ages.

Together, let's crack the Elisha Code and become participants in the next great end-times revival—a revival marked by a double portion of Christ's miraculous anointing.

Let the quest begin!

THE FIRE ON THE ROAD TO EMMAUS

And they said to one another, "Did not our
heart burn within us while He talked with us
on the road, and while He opened
the Scriptures to us?"
(Luke 24:32, NKJV)

Is there a conversation in the Bible that you wish you could listen in on? How about the conversation between Mary and Joseph when she announced she was pregnant? What about the discussion the disciples had after Jesus stilled the storm on the Sea of Galilee? Or that night when Peter got out of the boat and began walking on the water? Oh, to have been there—to have seen the disciples' astonishment and to have heard their words!

Luke tells us of a conversation two downcast Jesus-followers had on the road to Emmaus on the afternoon of the first resurrection Sunday.

So it was, while they conversed and reasoned, that Jesus Himself drew near and went with them. But their eyes were restrained, so that they did not know Him.

> And He said to them, "What kind of conversation
> is this that you have with one another as you walk and
> are sad?" (Luke 24:15–17, NKJV)

Jesus patiently listens as they speak of their dashed hopes and shattered dreams—dreams and hopes that ended with the crucifixion of the man they thought was the long-awaited Messiah. They go on to report that some of their women folk who had gone to his tomb had seen a vision of angels who announced this prophet from Nazareth was in fact alive. What were they to make of all this?

> Then He said to them, "O foolish ones, and slow of
> heart to believe in all that the prophets have spoken!
> Ought not the Christ to have suffered these things
> and to enter into His glory?" And beginning at Moses
> and all the Prophets, He expounded to them in all
> the Scriptures the things concerning Himself. (Luke
> 24:25–27, NKJV)

Certainly, that was a conversation we all wish we could have eavesdropped on. Specifically, what Scriptures did Jesus draw on as he expounded concerning himself? Let's keep in mind this was decades before any of the books of the New Testament canon were written.

Surely, Jesus would have drawn on Isaiah 53 as he spoke of his suffering. What about the Psalms? Many of them resound with a prophetic, Messianic ring. To a degree, we can imagine what some of those Old Testament references might be. For example, we know that Peter quoted verbatim from both Psalm 16 and Psalm 110 in his first sermon on the day of Pentecost. (See Acts 2:25–28 and Acts 2:34–35.) Did

Peter develop this understanding concerning these prophetic Scriptures on his own, or were these passages an integral part of Christ's teaching concerning himself during his post-resurrection ministry? Were they part of the discussion on that eventful resurrection Sunday walk?

Though the content of the Road to Emmaus discourse remains hidden from us, it is possible to tease out some of Christ's teaching concerning himself and his ministry by examining other passages in both the New and Old Testament.

According to Luke, Cleopas and his companion were initially unable to recognize Jesus when he walked with them on the road: *"But their eyes were restrained, so that they did not know Him"* (Luke 24:16, NKJV).

Two disciples—men who had previously spent time with Jesus—were blind to their Lord and Savior. Why was this the case? Undoubtedly, Jesus looked different. A brutal death followed by a supernatural resurrection must have brought significant changes to his physical appearance. A lifelong friend or relative may look startlingly different after a severe trauma or illness. Surely, this accounts for some of the disciples' inability to recognize Jesus.

But this inability to recognize Jesus extended beyond his physical appearance. It had a spiritual dimension. They were unable to recognize that Jesus was the Christ—the long-awaited Messiah promised to them in their Scriptures. After all, this was what the conversation on the road was all about. It was Jesus revealing himself to these two men through the written Word of Moses and the Prophets.

Do we suffer from the same spiritual blindness? Do we need an eye-opening experience with the Lord and his Word? This lack of perception inhibits our walk with our Savior. We think we know the Word of God. But like these disciples of old, have our eyes been veiled as we read the Scriptures? Do we have a wrong set of expectations?

Many Christ-followers have never read the Old Testament—the first three quarters of their Bibles. Similarly, many Sunday sermons focus exclusively on texts drawn from the New Testament. How can we say we know the Word when we neglect the only Scriptures that Jesus knew and studied?

Something transpires when we immerse ourselves in God's Word. Hearts and minds are transformed when the Word comes alive.

But let's not fool ourselves. If we don't understand the Word, or handle it incorrectly, we gain nothing. Worse yet, we deceive ourselves, pride inflates our minds, and we lead others astray. The Pharisees knew and followed the letter of the Law (the Word), but often they were devoid of the Spirit. The same self-deception can happen to us unless the Holy Spirit lights the way. Christ's parable of the Sower and the seed plays out in real time to this present moment. The living Word must root in us to bear fruit.

So, when did the light come on for Cleopas and his friend? When did recognition occur?

> Now it came to pass, as He sat at the table with them, that He took bread, blessed and broke it, and gave it to them. Then their eyes were opened and they knew Him; and He vanished from their sight. (Luke 24:30–31, NKJV)

Jesus was recognized when he broke bread with these two disciples. In that moment, they had their most intimate view of the living Christ.

Imagine the scene as Jesus picks up the bread. For the first time his hands come into full view. They gasp—awestruck at the sight of the nail scars. Who else could this be? It must be none but their Savior! He offers thanks to his Father. With wounded hands, he tears the loaf and offers them a portion.

Like Thomas, who will have a similar encounter nine days later, they are beyond astonished. Imagine them humbled— dropping to their knees before their Lord.

And then he is gone.

Only one thing remains. The fire remains. It remains within them.

> And they said to one another, "Did not our heart burn within us while He talked with us on the road, and while He opened the Scriptures to us?" (Luke 24:32, NKJV)

It's the same fire we must catch. The match was struck on the road to Emmaus. In the hearts of these two disciples, dying embers of hope began to glow as Jesus opened the Scriptures. Fifty days later, those embers would burst into open flame on the Day of Pentecost.

> And suddenly there came a sound from heaven, as of a rushing mighty wind, and it filled the whole house where they were sitting. Then there appeared to them divided tongues, as of fire, and one sat upon each of them. And they were all filled with the Holy Spirit and began to speak with other tongues, as the Spirit gave them utterance. (Acts 2:2–4, NKJV)

Are you ready to catch the fire?

2

THE RETURN OF THE DYNAMIC DUO

When they had crossed, Elijah said to Elisha,
"Tell me, what can I do for you
before I am taken from you?"
"Let me inherit a double portion of your spirit,"
Elisha replied.
"You have asked a difficult thing," Elijah said,
"yet if you see me when I am taken from you, it
will be yours—otherwise, it will not."
(2 Kings 2:9–10)

The more things change, the more they stay the same.[1] This common expression captures within it the seed truth that history tends to repeat itself. Human nature, social norms, and patterns of behavior stay the same across the continuum of time and space. Consequently, though the individual players, time, and location may differ, outcomes frequently are the same or fall into a familiar pattern. For this very reason, Bible stories remain relevant today, despite being written ages ago for people of a different language and culture.

---

[1] "Plus ça change, plus c'est la même chose," Jean-Baptiste Alphonse Karr, 1849.

In today's culture when we use the term *dynamic duo*, several pictures or scenarios immediately spring to mind. Batman and Robin from DC Comics popularized the term, but throughout history and within our own experience we have all encountered dynamic duos—individuals who work together well to accomplish a common purpose.

Can we identify dynamic duos in the Old Testament? We certainly can. Moses and his young successor Joshua spring to mind.

The prophets Elijah and Elisha are a dynamic duo whose miraculous powers and exploits rival the adventures of the finest superheroes in the Marvel Universe. First-century Jewish teens reading accounts of their miraculous feats would be immediately drawn to them. Furthermore, the last book of the Old Testament ends with the promise of Elijah's return.

> See, I will send the prophet Elijah to you before that great and dreadful day of the LORD comes. He will turn the hearts of the parents to their children, and the hearts of the children to their parents; or else I will come and strike the land with total destruction. (Malachi 4:5–6)

And if Elijah is returning, then Elisha, or an Elisha-like figure, cannot be far behind. As the New Testament era dawns, the stage is set for the return of the dynamic duo. There is nothing quite like a sequel. In this case it's a prophetic, dynamic-duo sequel that returns after an absence of about seven centuries. Imagine the anticipation.

Is it any wonder then that Elijah's name appears twenty-eight times in the Gospels? Aside from Peter, none of the apostles are named as frequently as Elijah. It is quite extraordinary for a hero from a previous era to be referenced so frequently. Yet the expectation of Elijah's arrival was palpable. Jesus was often incorrectly identified as the Elijah who is to come.[2] With the start of Christ's ministry, and his demonstration of miraculous powers, the burning question within the first-century Jewish community was "Has Elijah returned?"

The eleventh chapter of Matthew's Gospel answers that question directly. Jesus identifies who the new Elijah—the second Elijah—really is.

> And when John had heard in prison about the works of Christ, he sent two of his disciples and said to Him, "Are You the Coming One, or do we look for another?"
>
> Jesus answered and said to them, "Go and tell John the things which you hear and see: The blind see and the lame walk; the lepers are cleansed and the deaf hear; the dead are raised up and the poor have the gospel preached to them. And blessed is he who is not offended because of Me."
>
> As they departed, Jesus began to say to the multitudes concerning John: "What did you go out into the wilderness to see? A reed shaken by the wind? But what did you go out to see? A man clothed in soft garments? Indeed, those who wear soft clothing are in kings' houses. But what did you go out to see? A prophet? Yes, I say to you, and more than a prophet. For this is he of whom it is written:
>
>> 'Behold, I send My messenger before Your face, Who will prepare Your way before You.'
>
> "Assuredly, I say to you, among those born of women there has not risen one greater than John the

---

[2] Matthew 16:13–14

Baptist; but he who is least in the kingdom of heaven is greater than he. And from the days of John the Baptist until now the kingdom of heaven suffers violence, and the violent take it by force. For all the prophets and the law prophesied until John. And if you are willing to receive it, he is Elijah who is to come. He who has ears to hear, let him hear!" (Matthew 11:2–15, NKJV)

So, there we have the answer to the question on everyone's mind at that time. John the Baptist *is Elijah who is to come.* The first member of the New Testament dynamic duo has been identified.

What does Jesus' identification of John the Baptist as the new Elijah really mean? It does not mean John is the reincarnation of Elijah. Elijah's body was whisked away to heaven in a whirlwind on a chariot of fire.[3] Centuries later, he returned with Moses to meet with Jesus on the Mount of Transfiguration.[4]

Clearly, John and Elijah are two distinct persons from two distinct historical eras. In fact, when he was questioned about his identity, John denied being the Christ or Elijah.[5] However, Jesus rightly identified John the Baptist as moving and ministering in the spirit of Elijah. He fulfilled the prophecy of Malachi.[6]

Elijah's ministry was a ministry of repentance. His assignment from the LORD was to draw the backslidden people of Israel (the northern kingdom) back to worshipping the one true God. Israel had fallen into the grievous sin of idolatry under

---

[3] 2 Kings 2:11–12

[4] Matthew 17:1–13, Mark 9:2–13, Luke 9:28–36

[5] John 1:19–28

[6] "See, I will send the prophet Elijah to you before that great and dreadful day of the LORD comes. He will turn the hearts of the parents to their children, and the hearts of the children to their parents; or else I will come and strike the land with total destruction." (Malachi 4:5–6)

the rule of King Ahab and his evil consort Jezebel. Many had bowed their knees to Baal, the male fertility god, and partaken in the worship of the female deity Ashtoreth.

John the Baptist had a similar assignment. He too was to draw the Jewish nation back to God. But in the New Testament era, the sins of the nation were of a more subtle nature. The worship of Yahweh had become cold and formal, while the sinful heart was unchanged.

> The LORD says:
> "These people come near to me with their mouth and honor me with their lips, but their hearts are far from me. Their worship of me is based on merely human rules they have been taught." (Isaiah 29:13)

This corrupt condition of the heart is what John came to address. He did so with a clarion call to repentance followed by baptism. Furthermore, he insisted no one could claim safety from the coming wrath due to their lineage or national heritage.

> Produce fruit in keeping with repentance. And do not think you can say to yourselves, "We have Abraham as our father." I tell you that out of these stones God can raise up children for Abraham. The ax is already at the root of the trees, and every tree that does not produce good fruit will be cut down and thrown into the fire. (Matthew 3:8–10)

What root was John attacking with the above statement? He was hacking away at the presumption of salvation by virtue of national origin. The Sadducees and Pharisees who John was addressing trusted in their Jewish heritage as being sufficient for eternal salvation.

Apparently, your birth certificate doesn't qualify you for entrance into the kingdom of God. God is looking for a repentant heart—a changed heart.

With his words, John was laying the groundwork for Jesus' core message of salvation through regeneration. We must be born again, as Jesus revealed in his conversation with Nicodemus.[7] And the first step in that regenerative process begins with repentance, initially championed by John,[8] reiterated by Jesus,[9] and preached by the apostles.[10]

Today, we speak of disruptive technology changing the way business and society operate. John's message was disruptive theology. His message attempted to completely change how the Jewish society of that time viewed their relationship with God. Many Jewish people saw themselves as citizens in God's kingdom simply because they were children of Abraham. John's mission was to shatter that misperception. Something more was needed then, and it is still needed now. Salvation begins with a repentant heart. And like Elijah of old, John was calling the nation to repent and turn back to God.

Jesus addressed the same topic in his John 8:12–59 temple discourse with the Jewish religious leadership. In that heated discussion, Jesus' opponents trumpeted their Abrahamic pedigree, while rejecting the testimony of the Son of God. God is always looking for the fruits of repentance in our lives. But there was an absence of fruit in these religious leaders.

It was John the Baptist who first raised this issue with the Pharisees and Sadducees. If we are not simply born into the kingdom by natural birth, as the religious leadership claimed, how then do we gain entrance? Jesus provides the answer:

---

[7] John 3:1–21
[8] Matthew 3:1–2, Mark 1:4, Luke 3:2–3
[9] Matthew 4:17, Mark 1:14–15
[10] Acts 2:36–39, Acts 3:19

> Very truly I tell you, no one can enter the kingdom of
> God unless they are born of water and the Spirit. Flesh
> gives birth to flesh, but the Spirit gives birth to spirit.
> You should not be surprised at my saying, "You must
> be born again." (John 3:5– 7)

This disruptive theology was introduced by John and advanced to the next level through the ministry of Jesus. John and Jesus truly worked as a dynamic duo. Furthermore, all four Gospel writers recognized John's foundational contribution. It's striking that though each Gospel is focused on the life and ministry of Jesus, none of the Gospel writers begin their account with Jesus. They all begin with John. He truly was the forerunner and the way-maker for our Savior.

Many of the underpinnings of the Christian faith were introduced by John. Repentance followed by baptism is a prime example. Baptism, inspired by the Jewish *mikvah,* a ceremonial washing rooted in the Five Books of Moses, was an innovation introduced and popularized by John. Baptism represents a soul-transforming innovation that was, with only slight modification, incorporated directly into Christ's teaching and the Great Commission.

> "Go therefore and make disciples of all the nations,
> baptizing them in the name of the Father and of the
> Son and of the Holy Spirit, teaching them to observe
> all things that I have commanded you; and lo, I am
> with you always, even to the end of the age." Amen.
> (Matthew 28:19–20, NKJV)

Baptism is a living picture of new birth. It is the defining symbol and sacrament of the born-again experience. John laid the groundwork for the gospel of Christ. He worked like a bulldozer leveling the way for Christ.[11] He destroyed the argument that salvation was race-based, and in so doing he paved the way for Jesus' teaching on spiritual rebirth.

It logically follows that if salvation is not based on lineage or race, but rather on a spiritual rebirth, then that experience of rebirth is open to all humanity and not the sole domain of the Jewish people.

Both John and Jesus were looking for fruit—the transformative fruit of repentance.[12] And through the work of the Holy Spirit, that fruit could be found among both Jews and Gentiles. It was no longer confined to the Jewish nation. All could potentially be grafted into the vine through faith in Jesus.

Jesus identified John the Baptist as the new Elijah. Who then is the new Elisha?

---

[11] Matthew 3:3

[12] Matthew 3:8, Matthew 7:15–20, Matthew 21:33–46

3

THE MIRACULOUS POWER OF THE NEW ELISHA

> *Then he took the mantle of Elijah*
> *that had fallen from him,*
> *and struck the water, and said,*
> *"Where is the LORD God of Elijah?"*
> *And when he also had struck the water,*
> *it was divided this way and that;*
> *and Elisha crossed over.*
> (2 Kings 2:14, NKJV)

What defines you? We commonly identify people by their occupation or profession, so we speak of Bob the plumber, Maryanne the nurse, and Tom the teacher.

The Old Testament prophets played a unique role in the plan of God for his people. But unlike angels sent from heaven, they were the LORD's earthbound messengers—frail human agents sent to his wayward children. Frequently, they heralded a message of repentance, and they used various means to communicate the word of the LORD. Many of them were writers, and their writings became an integral part of the Holy Scriptures. Isaiah, Jeremiah, and Amos are examples of these author-prophets who continue to influence lives today through the written Word.

Elijah and Elisha are prime examples of the non-literary prophets. They did not pen any of the books of the Bible, though their deeds are recorded in the Scriptures so we can learn from their ministry and example. What made this prophetic duo unique were the miraculous signs that accompanied their ministry. Specifically, Elisha the prophet was defined by his miracle-working power. The LORD granted his request for a double portion of Elijah's miracle-working anointing.

But there is more to Elisha's miraculous signs than a simple display of God's power. In scope and sequence, Elisha's miracles run parallel to the miracles of Jesus in a most remarkable way.

However, before we consider the miracles of Jesus and Elisha, we should first be aware that their names are identical in meaning. In his commentary on 1 & 2 Kings, Iain W. Provan makes the following statement:

> …that the names "Joshua," "Elisha," and "Jesus" have essentially the same meaning ("God saves"), and that John the Baptist is so clearly identified in the Gospels with Elijah, it is intriguing that more is not explicitly made in the NT of the Jesus-Elisha connection.[1]

With these words, Provan has clearly identified the Jesus-Elisha connection that is at the heart of the Elisha Code. The first clue in interpreting the Elisha Code is found in the names of these two Bible characters. Both men are identified as saviors of their people.

---

[1] Iain W. Provan, *1 & 2 Kings*, Understanding the Bible Commentary Series. Accordance Bible Software electronic ed. (Grand Rapids, MI: Baker Books, 2012), 234.

The second clue or identifying marker comes in the miracles they performed.

Let's begin by looking at the first miracle of Elisha's public ministry.

> The people of the city said to Elisha, "Look, our lord, this town is well situated, as you can see, but the water is bad and the land is unproductive."
>
> "Bring me a new bowl," he said, "and put salt in it." So they brought it to him.
>
> Then he went out to the spring and threw the salt into it, saying, "This is what the LORD says: 'I have healed this water. Never again will it cause death or make the land unproductive.'" And the water has remained pure to this day, according to the word Elisha had spoken. (2 Kings 2:19–22)

There is a striking similarity between Elisha's first public miracle and Jesus' first miracle—his turning of water into wine as recorded in John 2:1–12. Both miracles involve the transformation of water—foul water into good water by Elisha, and good water into amazing wine by Jesus.

Both men act at the request of others. Both solve the problem before them by unexpected means.

Jericho is located on the plain of the Jordan River near the very saline waters of the Dead Sea. Why was the water bad and the land unproductive? The obvious answer is the high salt content in the soil and water. But what does Elisha do? He asks for a new bowl full of salt.

Can you imagine the consternation of the onlookers as this rookie prophet throws a bowl full of salt into this alkaline spring? Can you hear them muttering, "Good grief! How will that help?"

But Elisha spoke the word of the LORD: *"I have healed this water. Never again will it cause death or make the land unproductive."*

In the same way, Jesus, the Word incarnate, spoke transformation over the contents of six twenty-to-thirty-gallon stone jars at the Cana wedding. Imagine the astonishment of the servants who, having poured in water, moments later draw out the finest of wines.[2]

This miraculous sign points to the divine nature of the Messiah. He not only duplicates the Elisha miracles but elevates them to a new level. Furthermore, Jesus has been busy transforming the contents of earthen vessels—human vessels—since that time to this present moment.

Which of Elisha's miracles do believers most readily recall? Undoubtedly, it is the healing of the leper Naaman (2 Kings 5). The story of this Syrian general is frequently taught in Sunday School, and occasionally it forms the text for a Sunday sermon. From Elisha's long series of miracles, pastors and teachers most often cite this account of a healed leper.

In Matthew's Gospel, following the Sermon on the Mount, the first miracle Jesus performs is the healing of a man with leprosy.

When Jesus came down from the mountainside, large crowds followed him. A man with leprosy came and knelt before him and said, "Lord, if you are willing, you can make me clean."

Jesus reached out his hand and touched the man. "I am willing," he said. "Be clean!" Immediately he was cleansed of his leprosy. Then Jesus said to him, "See that you don't tell anyone. But go, show yourself to

---

[2] John 2:1–12

the priest and offer the gift Moses commanded, as a testimony to them." (Matthew 8:1–4)

This miracle acted as a signal—a beacon of hope. A new era had dawned. Surely, the prophets of old had returned. After a long absence, they had returned in spirit and power. Those who were alert to the Scriptures could read the signs of the times. The first sign was visible in the transformed body of this leper. The incurable leper had been cured!

Surely the final words of the prophet Malachi were being fulfilled:

> See, I will send the prophet Elijah to you before that great and dreadful day of the LORD comes. He will turn the hearts of the parents to their children, and the hearts of the children to their parents; or else I will come and strike the land with total destruction. (Malachi 4:5–6)

The ministry of John the Baptist was the fulfilment of this prophecy, and now Jesus the miracle worker was on the scene duplicating the wonders of Elisha's ministry. The Old Testament dynamic duo had returned, and the string of miracles recorded in Matthew chapters eight through ten bears witness to this thesis. Each successive miracle acts as a signpost helping us to crack the Elisha Code.

Before we continue our look at these signposts, a word of clarification is warranted. When we consider the return of Elijah and Elisha in New Testament times, we should not view this as a form of biblical reincarnation. The Bible does not support an intrusion of Hindu religious philosophy into Christian theology.

When Jesus says of John the Baptist *"he is the Elijah who is to come"* (Matthew 11:14, CSB), Jesus is speaking metaphorically as he so often did. Other examples of Jesus employing metaphors are statements such as *"I am the bread of life"* (John 6:35) or *"I am the gate for the sheep"* (John 10:7).

In clear and direct language, Jesus was stating that John was the prophetic fulfillment of Malachi 4:5–6, the last passage of the Old Testament covenant.

John the Baptist's link to Elijah is best summed up in the words of the angel Gabriel, spoken to John's father, Zechariah, before the conception of this New Testament prophet:

> He will bring back many of the people of Israel to the Lord their God. And he will go on before the Lord, in the spirit and power of Elijah, to turn the hearts of the parents to their children and the disobedient to the wisdom of the righteous—to make ready a people prepared for the Lord. (Luke 1:16–17)

Matthew immediately follows up his account of the healing of the leper with the healing of the centurion's servant (Matthew 8:5–13). Again, there is an unmistakable link here. Elisha healed Naaman, a foreign military leader, of leprosy. Similarly, Jesus, the New Testament healing prophet, after healing a leper, commends the great faith of a foreign military leader before going on to heal this Roman centurion's servant.

The perceptive Jewish reader of Matthew's Gospel would be intrigued by this juxtaposition of events. But alas, because we may not be steeped in the Jewish Old Testament tradition, we can too easily breeze past these accounts and see no connection between what Jesus is doing and what Elisha did.

The second most frequently cited miracle of Elisha is the raising of the Shunammite's son from the dead. See 2 Kings

4:8–37. Again, there is a parallel story of bringing a child back to life in Matthew's Gospel.

> While he [Jesus] was saying this, a synagogue leader came and knelt before him and said, "My daughter has just died. But come and put your hand on her, and she will live." (Matthew 9:18)

The circumstances of the synagogue leader are strikingly similar to the plight of the Shunammite. In both cases, after the death of their child, they travel to their local healing prophet— respectively Elisha and Jesus—fall on their knees before him, and plead for the prophet's intervention. The healing prophet responds by traveling to their home, going alone into a private room, and raising the child back to life.

Is this similarity a coincidence? Perhaps. If there were two or three instances of similarity in the miracles of Elisha and Jesus, we could chalk it up to coincidence, but as we continue to explore further, we will see a distinct pattern developing. Remarkably many of the miracles of Jesus resemble the miracles of Elisha, though they often rise to a new or higher level.

A classic example of this is Jesus' feeding of the five thousand. This miracle is found in each of the four Gospels. Furthermore, Matthew and Mark record not one, but two mass feedings, the feeding of the five thousand (Matthew 14:13–21, Mark 6:30–44) and the feeding of the four thousand (Matthew 15:29–39, Mark 8:1–9). But who performed the first miracle of mass feeding recorded in the Scriptures? If you guessed Elisha, give yourself a gold star.

> A man came from Baal Shalishah, bringing the man of God twenty loaves of barley bread baked from the first

ripe grain, along with some heads of new grain. "Give it to the people to eat," Elisha said.

"How can I set this before a hundred men?" his servant asked.

But Elisha answered, "Give it to the people to eat. For this is what the LORD says: 'They will eat and have some left over.'" Then he set it before them, and they ate and had some left over, according to the word of the LORD. (2 Kings 4:42–44)

Despite the much smaller scale of Elisha's miracle, we see a similar pattern in how this miracle rolls out when it is compared with Jesus' two crowd-feeding miracles. This includes the instructions given by the respective prophet and the response of their doubt-filled followers, and all three accounts conclude by referring to a surplus of leftovers.

Elisha also accomplished the only miracle of supernatural buoyancy found in the Hebrew Scriptures.

As one of them was cutting down a tree, the iron axhead fell into the water. "Oh no, my lord!" he cried out. "It was borrowed!"

The man of God asked, "Where did it fall?" When he showed him the place, Elisha cut a stick and threw it there, and made the iron float. "Lift it out," he said. Then the man reached out his hand and took it. (2 Kings 6:5–7)

This is a stunning miracle, but Jesus—Elisha's New Testament prophetic counterpart—elevates supernatural buoyancy to a whole new level. He walks on water (Matthew 14:22–33, Mark 6:45–52, John 6:16–21), and enables Peter to do the same.

There are also a few examples where Elisha's miracles are more stunning or perhaps personally relatable than those demonstrated by Jesus. Topping this list is Elisha's miracle of provision for a widow and her two boys who were about to be sold into slavery to cover an outstanding debt. At Elisha's command, the widow's jar of olive oil kept pouring golden liquid until there was sufficient to cover every debt and more left over to live on (see 2 Kings 4:1–7).

This miracle of provision is an appropriate match with Jesus' miracle in which he sent Peter to catch a fish. In the mouth of the fish was a four-drachma coin Peter was to use for paying the temple tax for himself and Jesus (see Matthew 17:24–27). Both miracles occur for the purpose of paying money that is owed, and while both miracles are stunning when you consider how such events could be possible, the story of the widow's ever-flowing jar resonates more strongly with our hearts because of this family's dire need.

In chapters eight through ten of his Gospel, Matthew is painting a portrait for his Jewish audience of Jesus the miracle-working prophet. It is a portrait that most closely resembles the works of the Old Testament prophet Elisha, and this portrait includes a miracle demonstrating Jesus' power over nature.

> Then he got into the boat and his disciples followed him. Suddenly a furious storm came up on the lake, so that the waves swept over the boat. But Jesus was sleeping. The disciples went and woke him, saying, "Lord, save us! We're going to drown!"
>
> He replied, "You of little faith, why are you so afraid?" Then he got up and rebuked the winds and the waves, and it was completely calm.

The men were amazed and asked, "What kind of man is this? Even the winds and the waves obey him!" (Matthew 8:23–27)

Elisha also has a power-over-nature miracle in his repertoire. During a time of war with Moab, he was called upon to prophesy as the armies of Edom, Israel, and Judah faced death from thirst in the sun-scorched desert.

While the harpist was playing, the hand of the LORD came on Elisha and he said, "This is what the LORD says: I will fill this valley with pools of water. For this is what the LORD says: You will see neither wind nor rain, yet this valley will be filled with water, and you, your cattle and your other animals will drink. This is an easy thing in the eyes of the LORD; he will also deliver Moab into your hands. (2 Kings 3:15b–18)

Elisha's word came true the next morning as the desert of Edom was filled with water.[3]

The question the disciples asked in that boat more than two thousand years ago still resonates today. *What kind of man is this? Even the winds and the waves obey him!"* (Matthew 8:27).

If we are going to rightly interpret the Elisha Code, we need a more accurate picture of Jesus. And to get that accurate picture we need eyes that see beyond the shallow surface. We need to comprehend the Old Testament roots of our faith more fully, or we will remain blind to aspects of what Jesus has done and is about to do through his followers in our day.

---

[3] "The next morning, about the time for offering the sacrifice, there it was—water flowing from the direction of Edom! And the land was filled with water" (2 Kings 3:20).

In his commentary, Iain Provan states that throughout church history "the typological significance of Elisha in relation to Jesus has been downplayed."[4]

Now is a good time to correct that oversight.

---

[4] Iain W. Provan, *1 & 2 Kings,* Understanding the Bible Commentary Series. Accordance electronic ed. (Grand Rapids, MI: Baker Books, 2012), 234.

4

OPENING BLIND EYES

*In that day the deaf will hear
the words of the scroll,
and out of gloom and darkness the eyes of the blind will see.*
(Isaiah 29:18)

I n 1546, the English writer and poet John Heywood penned this proverb, "There are none so blind as those who will not see."[1]

Heywood's proverb is as relevant to our times as it was in his day. The most damaging condition modern humanity suffers from is spiritual blindness. But alas, this condition has been afflicting humans since we exited Eden.

Perhaps no biblical account portrays spiritual blindness better than the story of Elisha and his servant when they were trapped in the besieged city of Samaria. On the first morning of the siege, Elisha's servant panicked when he saw the foreign army, but the prophet responded with these words:

---

[1] "Who wrote the proverb 'There are…'", *Quizz Club*, (https://quizzclub.com/trivia/who-wrote-the-proverb-there-are-none-so-blind-as-those-who-will-not-see/answer/439985/)

> "Don't be afraid," the prophet answered. "Those who are with us are more than those who are with them."
>
> And Elisha prayed, "Open his eyes, LORD, so that he may see." Then the LORD opened the servant's eyes, and he looked and saw the hills full of horses and chariots of fire all around Elisha. (2 Kings 6:16–17)

As is so often the case, the servant was blind to the spiritual realm. Today, the servants of God suffer from the same short-sightedness. It took the prayer of Elisha to open the servant's eyes. In our day, it also takes the Holy Spirit and present-day prophets to open our eyes.

This eye-opening miracle was paired with a mass-blinding miracle on an unprecedented scale.

> As the enemy came down toward him, Elisha prayed to the LORD, "Strike this army with blindness." So he struck them with blindness, as Elisha had asked.
>
> Elisha told them, "This is not the road and this is not the city. Follow me, and I will lead you to the man you are looking for." And he led them to Samaria. (2 Kings 6:18–19)

Elisha led the enemy army into the presence of the king of Israel in the heart of the capital. The king then inquired if he should slaughter his enemies. But Elisha counseled kindness rather than retribution, and a feast was prepared for the Aramean army. This act of unprecedented grace and generosity led to a time of peace between these two warring nations (2 Kings 6:23).

Eight centuries before Christ, Elisha's advice to the king puts into practice the words of Jesus from his Sermon on the Mount.

But to you who are listening I say: Love your enemies, do good to those who hate you, bless those who curse you, pray for those who mistreat you. If someone slaps you on one cheek, turn to them the other also. If someone takes your coat, do not withhold your shirt from them. Give to everyone who asks you, and if anyone takes what belongs to you, do not demand it back. Do to others as you would have them do to you. (Luke 6:27–31)

There is an uncanny link between Elisha, the Old Testament prophet, and Jesus, his New Testament counterpart. Both men see beyond the natural realm to the astonishment of the people of their day, and both prophets counsel kindness rather than revenge in dealing with enemies.

Though there are many outstanding miracles recorded in the Old Testament, there is no account of the physically blind receiving their sight. Yet, time after time in the Gospels, Jesus restored sight to the blind.[2] These physical miracles were signposts pointing to an even more significant restoration of sight: the restoration of spiritual eyesight; eyesight that allows us to see who Jesus truly is and what he is doing.

The account of Jesus healing the blind man at the Pool of Siloam is entirely about opening the eyes of those who are both physically and spiritually blind. (See John 9.) The man who received his sight was blind from birth. This was not simply a miracle of restoration. It was a creative miracle, on par with the Adam and Eve account in Genesis 2, as Jesus so aptly demonstrated.

---

[2] Matthew 12:22, Matthew 15:30, Mark 8:22–26, Mark 10:46–52, Luke 7:21, John 9

> "While I am in the world, I am the light of the world."
>
> After saying this, he spit on the ground, made some mud with the saliva, and put it on the man's eyes. "Go," he told him, "wash in the Pool of Siloam" (this word means "Sent"). So the man went and washed, and came home seeing. (John 9:5–7)

Jesus opened the eyes of the blind man, but as the story continues, we see he is unable to open the eyes of the spiritually blind Pharisees. John Heywood's proverb proves true: "There are none so blind as those who will not see."

The Pharisees in this account were willfully blind. Many today suffer from the same willful blindness. Due to their stubborn hearts, they are unable to see who Jesus truly is.

The entirety of John 9 is about seeing—seeing and recognizing who Jesus is. The miracle of the man blind from birth receiving his sight should have alerted the Pharisees and temple authorities to the divine nature of Jesus, the miracle worker. But the Pharisees could not see past the fact this miracle had been wrought on the Sabbath. The miracle worker had violated the Sabbath, so they reasoned that he must be a sinner and unworthy of respect.

> Then they turned again to the blind man, "What have you to say about him? It was your eyes he opened."
>
> The man replied, "He is a prophet." (John 9:17)

The healed blind man stated what was patently obvious to him. He recognized that he had been touched by the hand of God. He saw Jesus as a prophet. All of Israel was waiting expectantly for a prophet—one who would once again demonstrate the power of the Almighty. Surely, restoring sight to one who was born blind was a demonstration of this power. But the Pharisees questioned the validity of the miracle and the miracle worker.

Why were many Pharisees so spiritually blind? Despite the evidence of multiple miracles, they were unwilling to recognize Jesus as a prophet. But this blindness was not a new condition. They had already rejected John the Baptist, the forerunner of the Messiah. They refused to recognize John as a prophet too. (See Matthew 21:25–27.)

And why did most Pharisees reject John the Baptist? The simple answer is because John preached a message of repentance. Repentance requires an acknowledgement of sin and a turning away from it. But the Pharisees, like many people nowadays, saw themselves as righteous already. They were blind to their sin. Furthermore, repentance requires humility, a character quality they shunned in favor of obstinate pride—pride in their self-professed righteousness.

Because the Pharisees did not recognize the first prophet, John, they were blind to the second prophet, Jesus. But Jesus was far more than a prophet. As his name implies, he was and is the Savior of the world. But the proud and the self-righteous have no felt need for a Savior. They see themselves as saved already—saved through their own efforts. In their own eyes—their spiritually blind eyes—they see no need for a Savior.

This same spiritual blindness afflicts many in both the church and society today. The cure for spiritual blindness is repentance and rebirth by the power of the Holy Spirit. That was the message of our two New Testament prophets, John the Baptist and Jesus.

The prophetic role of Christ is often ignored or downplayed in the church today. But the early reformers recognized this crucial function in Jesus' ministry. In his explanation of the second article of the Apostles' Creed, Luther writes:

> Christ was anointed to be my Prophet, Priest, and King.
> As my Prophet, He revealed Himself by word and deed,
> and by the preaching of the Gospel still reveals Himself
> as the Son of God and the Redeemer of the world.[3]

A gospel message that is preached without a call to repentance is not a gospel message at all. Coming to faith in Jesus requires—no, demands—repentance. Real repentance is real change. Change from the inside out. Change that is deep, meaningful, and evident in daily life.

John demanded change from those who came to be baptized, whatever their station in life, and that included Pharisees who in their pride believed no change was required (see Matthew 3:1–12).

Furthermore, we should not see repentance simply as a one-time occurrence. Yes, it is the vital starting point in our walk of faith,[4] but true repentance goes far beyond that. Repentance must be incorporated into our way of life—a life of continual turning away from sin and living in humble service to our Savior-King.[5]

Though the blind man received his sight, the Pharisees persisted in their spiritual blindness, even though the miracle-working Savior was standing before them.

---

[3] *Luther's Small Catechism: A Handbook of Christian Doctrine* (St. Louis, MO: Concordia Publishing House), 107.

[4] "Peter replied, 'Repent and be baptized, every one of you, in the name of Jesus Christ for the forgiveness of your sins. And you will receive the gift of the Holy Spirit'" (Acts 2:38).

[5] "If we claim to be without sin, we deceive ourselves and the truth is not in us. If we confess our sins, he is faithful and just and will forgive us our sins and purify us from all unrighteousness. If we claim we have not sinned, we make him out to be a liar and his word is not in us" (1 John 1:8–10).

Jesus said, "For judgment I have come into this world, so that the blind will see and those who see will become blind."

Some Pharisees who were with him heard him say this and asked, "What? Are we blind too?"

Jesus said, "If you were blind, you would not be guilty of sin; but now that you claim you can see, your guilt remains." (John 9:39–41)

For the Pharisees of Jesus' day and the spiritually blind of our day, this maxim holds true: If we don't recognize the prophet, we won't recognize the Savior.

Jesus' words remain relevant today:

Whoever welcomes a prophet as a prophet will receive a prophet's reward, and whoever welcomes a righteous person as a righteous person will receive a righteous person's reward. (Matthew 10:41)

The voice of the prophet is needed today, just as it was in Jesus' day. A national call to repentance is needed now. Who will voice that call? Where are the prophets for our time?

The relative absence of legitimate prophetic voices in the church today should trouble us. There was a four-hundred-year prophetic gap between the Old and New Testament—a gap when the Spirit of God was silent. But then suddenly John the Baptist and Jesus appeared on the scene. The first two chapters of Luke describe an astonishing flurry of Spirit-initiated activity as heaven set the great redemption story into motion. Will there be a similar flood of Spirit-directed activity before Christ's second coming?

It is clear from the Scriptures that prophets were active within the New Testament church, and furthermore, Paul considered them essential to the proper functioning of the body of Christ.

> So Christ himself gave the apostles, the prophets, the evangelists, the pastors and teachers, to equip his people for works of service, so that the body of Christ may be built up until we all reach unity in the faith and in the knowledge of the Son of God and become mature, attaining to the whole measure of the fullness of Christ. (Ephesians 4:11–13)

In Acts we read that there were numerous prophets active in the church. Some of them are listed by name. They include Agabus, Barnabas, Simeon called Niger, Lucius of Cyrene, Manaen, and Saul.[6] This Saul is also known as Paul, and he and Barnabas were commissioned by the church leadership in Antioch to go on the first great missionary journey (Acts 13:1–3).

Where would the church be today if these prophets had not spoken the word of the Lord over Paul and Barnabas? Would there be a church in Europe? Would we even know of the ministry of Paul? The New Testament church grew as it received prophetic direction from those who were attuned to hear the plans of God.

The church of God grows and flourishes when there are men and women who hear what the Spirit is saying, see what the Spirit is doing, and then declare it to the church and the world. That is the role of the prophet.

We need leaders with prophetic hindsight, insight, and foresight for the church to reach its full potential.

Prophetic vision is not always forward looking or predictive. Sometimes it looks back at events in the past and sees them

---

[6] Acts 11:27–28, Acts 13:1–3, Acts 15:32, Acts 21:8–10

with heaven-endowed clarity. For example, Jesus spoke to the Samaritan woman at the well about her past marriages and current living arrangement (John 4:15–19). As a result, the Samaritan woman immediately recognized Jesus as a prophet. This gift of prophetic hindsight was pivotal in this entire community coming to faith.

> Many of the Samaritans from that town believed in him because of the woman's testimony, "He told me everything I ever did." So when the Samaritans came to him, they urged him to stay with them, and he stayed two days. And because of his words many more became believers. (John 4:39–41)

The same prophetic hindsight is needed today to capture the attention of individuals and reach whole communities estranged from Christ and the gospel.

A word of caution is in order. Not all who call themselves prophets or apostles *are* prophets and apostles. A true prophet or apostle will be known by the fruit of their ministry, not by the self-styled handle on their business card. There have been false prophets throughout history. We should not be surprised when we see a raft of them emerge today. But the emergence of the counterfeit should not keep us from heeding those who genuinely hear from God and declare his word.

Paul's admonition to the Thessalonians remains valid:

> Do not quench the Spirit. Do not despise prophecies. Test all things; hold fast what is good. Abstain from every form of evil. (1 Thessalonians 5:19–22, NKJV)

Humility and service to others are the hallmarks of genuine faith. Pride and self-aggrandizement are flashing red lights signalling error and deception. Know the Scriptures, heed the Spirit, and proceed with caution. God guides those who humbly seek him. Jesus still opens the eyes of the blind, and he still uses prophetic voices to do just that.

The third key that helps us unlock the Elisha Code is prophetic vision or spiritual insight. It is vitally needed today.

5

A CALL FOR LITERARY PROPHETS

*Jesus performed many other signs
in the presence of his disciples,
which are not recorded in this book.
But these are written that you may believe that
Jesus is the Messiah, the Son of God,
and that by believing you may have life
in his name.*
(John 20:30–31)

As stated earlier, the Old Testament prophetic duo of Elijah and Elisha can be categorized as non-literary prophets, in contrast to a host of literary prophets such as Isaiah, Ezekiel, and Micah, who provided us with the Old Testament canon.

Like Elijah and Elisha, John the Baptist and Jesus are the premier non-literary prophets of the New Testament period. They wrote nothing for us to read. In fact, the memory of their incredible lives and deeds would undoubtedly have faded into obscurity without the work of four diligent publicists named Matthew, Mark, Luke, and John. Such is the indelible power of the written word.

Have literary prophets arisen in our time—in the era in which we live? There are ample reasons to believe the answer is yes. But before we look for examples of current or historic literary prophets, a point of clarification is required. This search for literary prophets is not about adding to the established canon of Holy Scripture. The literary prophets we are talking about simply draw people back into relationship with God. This, after all, was the primary goal of godly prophetic voices down through the ages. Often that involved challenging the norms, beliefs, and systems of the time.

In this respect, perhaps the greatest prophet of the last millennium was Martin Luther (1483–1546). He brought Europe out of the dark ages and into the glorious light of the gospel—a gospel that had been distorted almost beyond recognition by layers of institutional corruption, false doctrine, and a profound ignorance of the Holy Scriptures.

How did Luther bring about such a radical change? The answer lies primarily in his work as a literary prophet. Scholars and historians agree that foremost among his literary works is his translation of the Bible into German, the vernacular of the people of central Europe. Of course, this inspired translators in other lands to produce Bibles in their own local tongues. Suddenly, the Word of God was unleashed and active, changing hearts and lives across the continent, and the work of Bible translation continues to this day.

None of this would have taken place with such speed without the invention of Gutenberg's printing press, which for the first time made the Scriptures affordable and readily available. New technology presents new opportunities to transmit the gospel message. Are we effectively using the new technologies available to us to advance the redeeming message of Christ in the world?

In addition to translating the Bible, Luther authored a host of books, pamphlets, and tracts that expounded on biblical truth and exposed doctrinal error. Some of his views have been discredited, but many remain relevant.[1] He was a prophetic voice to his generation, and through his writing, his message still resounds five hundred years later.

Four centuries after Luther, in eastern Europe, another literary figure arose to challenge the religious and political thinking of his time. His name was Leo Tolstoy (1828–1910).

What might it take for peace to come today between Ukraine and Russia? What seems impossible with people is still possible with God.

What if Ukrainians and Russians would both rediscover the message of peace, forgiveness, and reconciliation in Tolstoy's *War & Peace*? Sadly, this book is currently banned in Ukraine because of the mistaken idea that it glorifies the Russian military.

After serving in the Crimean War as a young officer in the Russian army, Tolstoy became a committed pacifist. *War & Peace* never glorifies war, but rather, it accurately portrays how war often embitters our souls, dehumanizes us, and robs us of the love of neighbor. Ironically, the Russian Orthodox Church excommunicated Tolstoy in 1901, partially because he questioned their uncritical support for the Russian military.

Many see Tolstoy as a Russian Charles Dickens. Considered by many as the world's best novel, *War & Peace* overwhelms potential readers by its 1,400-page size. What surprised us as readers was how deeply Jesus' gospel message of forgiveness was woven into this book. God is mentioned 312 times in *War & Peace*. Outwardly, the book is about Napoleon's invasion of

---

[1] While we honor Martin Luther as a literary prophet used to further God's kingdom in the Reformation, we acknowledge the tragic nature of the antisemitism that Luther slipped into later in his ministry.

Russia, but at a deeper level, it is about human conflict and how the kingdom of God is the only solution.

The Russian Prince Andrei, who represents the glorification of war in *War & Peace*, initially despises forgiveness as just for women and children.[2] After being mortally wounded, Andrei learns to forgive his dying enemy Anatole Kuragin, and his ex-fiancée Natasha who almost ran off with Anatole. He notably commented:

> Compassion, love of our brothers, for those who love us and for those who hate us, love of our enemies; yes, that love which God preached on earth… and I did not understand—that is what made me sorry to part with life, that is what remained for me had I lived. But now it is too late. I know it![3]

Andrei asks his doctor to get him a copy of the Gospels, saying that he now has a new source of happiness which has something to do with the Gospels. After discovering the law of love, Andrei meets again with Natasha, who is devastated with guilt and shame:

> "Forgive me!" she whispered, raising her head and glancing at him. "Forgive me!"
>
> "I love you," said Prince Andrei…
>
> "Forgive…!"
>
> "Forgive what?" he asked.
>
> "Forgive me for what I have do-ne!" faltered Natasha in a scarcely audible, broken whisper, and began kissing his hand more rapidly, just touching it with her lips.

---

[2] Leo Tolstoy, *War and Peace* (Kindle Locations 19935-19936). Kindle Edition.
[3] Leo Tolstoy, *War and Peace* (Kindle Locations 22902-22903). Kindle Edition.

"I love you more, better than before," said Prince Andrei, lifting her face with his hand so as to look into her eyes.[4]

This novel could have been called *Love & Forgiveness*. Seventy-two times, Tolstoy talks about forgiveness in *War & Peace*. It was not just about the war with Napoleon, it was about the war between the sexes.

Another character in *War & Peace*, Pierre Bezukhov, is like a Russian Forrest Gump. He is a tragically comic figure who awkwardly stumbles into all the key moments of the Napoleonic conflict, unexpectedly acting as a savior figure and allowing us to observe the historic conflict in person, up close. Everything about him is unlikely, from him being an illegitimate son to becoming the wealthiest person in all of Russia. Through dreams and visions, Pierre discovers on Napoleon's battlefield that:

To love life is to love God. Harder and more blessed than all else is to love this life in one's sufferings, in innocent sufferings.[5]

Through discovering God, Pierre experiences a deep tranquility and happiness. He is no longer tormented by the meaninglessness of life:

…a simple answer was now always ready in his soul: "Because there is a God, that God without whose will not one hair falls from a man's head."[6]

---

[4] Leo Tolstoy, *War and Peace* (Kindle Locations 19935-19936). Kindle Edition.
[5] Leo Tolstoy, *War and Peace* (Kindle Locations 22902-22903). Kindle Edition.
[6] Leo Tolstoy, *War and Peace* (Kindle Locations 23761-23762). Kindle Edition.

Meeting God gave him such a new ability to listen that people regularly told Pierre their most intimate secrets. This deep listening was what caused the embittered princess Natasha to fall in love and marry him.

Tolstoy, a Russian aristocrat, became so enamoured with the Sermon on the Mount that he gave away all his wealth and chose to live like a peasant, tilling the land. When he decided to give up all of his authorial income, his wife threatened to divorce him, so he compromised by only giving away the money from any of his newly written books.

Tolstoy's book *The Kingdom of God Is Within You* so impacted Mahatma Gandhi that he gave it out to his followers. Gandhi was so impressed by Tolstoy's emphasis on the Sermon on the Mount (Matthew 5 to 7) that he read Jesus' famous Sermon every day for the rest of his life. Tolstoy's emphasis on nonviolent resistance formed the basis of Gandhi's campaign for Indian nationhood. Thus, through the influence of Tolstoy's writing, the entire subcontinent of India was transformed.

Martin Luther King Jr., after reading E. Stanley Jones' book on Gandhi, discovered the nonviolent key for his civil rights movement in America. So, the torch light of a peace-making gospel passed from a Russian author to India and on to America.

Tolstoy's passion for peace-making and forgiveness might even change Russia's President Putin, if he would only take the time to read Tolstoy's book.

The late British journalist and Christian apologist Malcolm Muggeridge deeply admired the genius of Tolstoy:

Tolstoy was one of those truly great men who come into the world at long intervals, and we need them, and we rightly continue to look to them just as the Russians do, despite all the changes that have happened.[7]

---

[7] Malcolm Muggeridge, "Leo Tolstoy," *A Third Testament* season 1, episode 1. https://www.youtube.com/watch?v=bzJMU7VE4Hk

What if instead of resenting Russia for its tragic invasion of the Ukraine, we, like Tolstoy, began to pray passionately for its transformation? Could we have faith to believe that Russia will become a Sermon on the Mount nation, overflowing with peacemakers like Tolstoy? Let's call out to God for such a miracle.

On this continent in 1852, Harriet Beecher Stowe wrote a novel that transfixed America. *Uncle Tom's Cabin* was the bestselling book in United States in the nineteenth century, surpassed only by the Bible.[8] Stowe was motivated by her deep Christian faith. Her book pricked the conscience of the nation, exposed the horrors of slavery, and fomented the upheaval that led to the American Civil War, which culminated in the emancipation of millions.

Martin Luther, Leo Tolstoy, and Harriet Beecher Stowe exemplify the incredible power of the printed page. Literary prophets are history shapers. They have transformed nations, and their influence remains to this day. We need more literary prophets—prophets filled with the courage of their convictions, prophets for our time.

The written word inspires faith—life-transforming faith. Perhaps John, the beloved, expressed this truth best when at the close of his Gospel he penned these immortal words: *"But these are written that you may believe that Jesus is the Messiah, the Son of God, and that by believing you may have life in his name"* (John 20:31).

---

[8] "Uncle Tom's Cabin," *Wikipedia*. https://en.wikipedia.org/wiki/Uncle_Tom%27s_Cabin, accessed March 1, 2023.

6

SAVING THE BEST TILL LAST

Up from the grave he arose;
With a mighty triumph o'er his foes;
He arose a victor from the dark domain,
And he lives forever, with his saints to reign.
He arose! He arose! Hallelujah! Christ arose![1]

Thus far in our examination of the ministry of Elisha and Jesus, we can see there are striking parallels in the miracles they worked.

- Their first public miracle was the transformation of water. Elisha turned a spring of foul water into good water at Jericho (2 Kings 2:19–22). Jesus turned water into wine at the wedding in Cana (John 2:1–12).
- Elisha healed Naaman the Syrian leper (2 Kings 5:1–19). Jesus healed a leper after delivering his Sermon on the Mount (Matthew 8:1–4).

---

[1] Robert Lowry, "Christ Arose," 1874 (public domain). https://hymnary.org/text/low_in_the_grave_he_lay_jesus_my_savior, accessed July 13, 2023.

- Elisha brought the Shunammite's son back to life (2 Kings 4:8-37), and Jesus brought the synagogue leader's daughter back to life (Matthew 9:18–26).
- Elisha miraculously fed a hundred men (2 Kings 4:42–44). Jesus miraculously fed a crowd of five thousand men (Matthew 14:13–21), and then a crowd of four thousand (Matthew 15:29–39).
- Both prophets demonstrated miracles of supernatural buoyancy. Elisha caused an iron axe-head to float (2 Kings 6:5–7), and Jesus walked on water (Matthew 14:22–33, Mark 6:45–52, John 6:15–21).
- Both men worked miracles of provision. A widow's jar of olive oil kept pouring and filled dozens of containers (2 Kings 4:1–7), and at Jesus' command Peter caught a fish with a gold coin in its mouth (Matthew 17:24–27).
- Both demonstrated power over nature. Elisha prophesied the arrival of water in the desert without wind or rain (2 Kings 3:15–18). Jesus stilled the wind and waves on the Sea of Galilee (Matthew 8:23–27).
- Elisha opened the spiritual eyes of his servant (2 Kings 6:16–17), and Jesus opened the eyes of the blind man at the Pool of Siloam (John 9:5–7), as well as numerous others.

When seen in tandem, this string of eight parallel miracles points to the arrival of the great Messianic prophet that Israel was longing for. Elisha's double anointing was being doubled yet again through the ministry of Jesus. The New Testament Elisha had arrived, and his name was Jesus of Nazareth.

Matthew deliberately framed his Gospel narrative so his Jewish readers could easily discern how Jesus duplicated and fulfilled the pattern established by the Old Testament miracle-working prophets.

When the disciples of John the Baptist arrived to inquire if Jesus was the long-awaited Messiah, how did he respond? He listed a string of miracles:

> Jesus replied, "Go back and report to John what you hear and see: The blind receive sight, the lame walk, those who have leprosy are cleansed, the deaf hear, the dead are raised, and the good news is proclaimed to the poor. Blessed is anyone who does not stumble on account of me." (Matthew 11:4–6)

Why did Jesus respond in this somewhat indirect, enigmatic way? With his answer, he was drawing the link between his current ministry and the miracle-working prophetic ministry of the Old Testament duo of Elijah and Elisha. When John's disciples leave, Jesus makes this abundantly clear to the crowd gathered around him by explicitly stating that John *"is the Elijah who is to come"* (Matthew 11:14, CSB).

For those who have ears to hear, the implications are clear. If the new Elijah is already here in the person of John, then the miracles of Jesus herald his arrival as the new Elisha. Furthermore, Jesus' answer implies that he is John the Baptist's successor, just as Elisha was Elijah's successor. With John imprisoned, the double anointing now rests on Jesus, and in his conversation with John's disciples he offers up his accomplishments as a miracle-worker as full proof of this prophetic transition.

The hallmark of Elisha's ministry was his double anointing (2 Kings 2:9). Elisha performed twice as many miracles as Elijah—more than thrice as many by some calculations. In his Gospel, Matthew signals that this double anointing rests on Jesus in a most unusual way. Generations of Bible scholars and apologists have puzzled over Matthew's double vision.

Repeatedly, Matthew reports on two men receiving miraculous help when the other Gospel writers report only one person receiving help.

The first example of this is found in Matthew's report on the restoration of two demon-possessed men in the region of the Gadarenes (Matthew 8:28–34). This corresponds closely with the report of what appears to be the same event in Mark's Gospel (Mark 5:1–20) and Luke's Gospel (Luke 8:26–39). Mark's account goes into considerably more detail, but Mark and Luke make no mention of a second man.

The second occurrence is found in Matthew's healing of two blind men (Matthew 9:27–31). Again, for the perceptive, this double healing serves as a sign of the double anointing now resting on Jesus.

The third example of Matthew's double vision occurs as Jesus is leaving Jericho on his last Passover pilgrimage to Jerusalem.

> Two blind men were sitting by the roadside, and when they heard that Jesus was going by, they shouted, "Lord, Son of David, have mercy on us!" (Matthew 20:30)

Similar accounts appear in Mark's Gospel (Mark 10:46-52) and Luke's Gospel (Luke 18:35-43). Again, Mark provides more detail by identifying the blind man as Bartimaeus. And yet again, Mark and Luke make no mention of a second man.

Finally, all four Gospel writers report on the feeding of the 5,000, but only Matthew and Mark include the feeding of the 4,000. Again, Matthew reports a double miracle, while Luke and John remain silent on the second miraculous feeding.

Bible scholars and apologists have come up with some sound reasons for these discrepancies in the four Gospels, which for the sake of brevity we will not explore here. But the following is one possible explanation:

We tend to see what we are looking for, and undoubtedly, this principle applies to Matthew as well. When we are watching for something, we will pick out the item or event we are searching for against a busy backdrop of other sights and events. We see it because we are watching for it. The words of Jesus ring true: *"seek and you will find…"* (Matthew 7:7).

A recent experience David Kitz had serves to illustrate this point. While walking along the shoreline of a marsh, he came upon a muskrat lodge protruding above the ice. He was fascinated by this discovery. After continuing further, he returned and then retraced his steps and found five more muskrat lodges. He had passed by these lodges minutes earlier but had noticed none of them. He saw them now because he was looking for them.

So, why did Matthew see and record his list of double miracles? Could it be because he was actively watching for evidence of a double anointing resting on Jesus, whereas the other Gospel writers had their attention fixed elsewhere? Matthew was expecting to see miracles in duplicate because he was keenly aware of the Old Testament dynamic duo and their prophetic narrative. He was familiar with Elisha's miracles, and now he was watching the same pattern of miracles repeated with a twofold impact. Yes, Elisha's double anointing was being doubled yet again.

Furthermore, Matthew was writing with his Jewish audience in mind—an audience that was familiar with and watching for the return of the voice and power of the Old Covenant prophets. He was writing to his people in a code they could readily decipher because they were steeped in Old Testament lore and primed to expect the arrival of their Messiah. Matthew was declaring to his countrymen that the prophetic power and anointing had returned first in the person of John the Baptist, and now through the ministry of Jesus. For this reason, his Gospel narrative directly cites more than forty Old Testament passages and alludes to many others.[2]

Like any great storyteller, Matthew saves the climax of the story until the end—just before the conclusion of his Gospel. And there is no greater climax to any story than the resurrection of Jesus. Again, in Matthew's account, there is a discernable link to resurrection in the end-of-life experiences of both Elisha and Jesus.

Elisha has his own post-death resurrection story. Like many of Elisha's miracles, it is an event without precedent in the Old Testament. Elisha's final miracle happened months or possibly years after his death.

> Elisha died and was buried.
> Now Moabite raiders used to enter the country every spring. Once while some Israelites were burying a man, suddenly they saw a band of raiders; so they threw the man's body into Elisha's tomb. When the body touched Elisha's bones, the man came to life and stood up on his feet. (2 Kings 13:20–21)

In his death Elisha brought forth life. How miraculous—how Christ-like!

In the same way Jesus, the New Testament Elisha, brought forth resurrection life when he died.

> And when Jesus had cried out again in a loud voice, he gave up his spirit.

---

[2] Krisan Marotta, "Matthew's Use of the Old Testamant," *Wednesday in the Word* (blog). October 26, 2020. https://www.wednesdayintheword.com/matthew-oldtestament/

> At that moment the curtain of the temple was torn in two from top to bottom. The earth shook, the rocks split and the tombs broke open. The bodies of many holy people who had died were raised to life. They came out of the tombs after Jesus' resurrection and went into the holy city and appeared to many people. (Matthew 27:50–53)

Again, Matthew is the only Gospel writer who reports this phenomenal event. Perhaps Matthew met with residents of Jerusalem who told him of their encounters with these resurrected holy people. Perhaps he or some of the other apostles had such an encounter.

Once more, we see a striking parallel between this final resurrection miracle of Jesus' earthly ministry, and the final resurrection miracle of Elisha. Of course, Christ's miracle in death is an amplified version of Elisha's posthumous resurrection miracle. Elisha brought only one man back to life, while Jesus brought many holy people up from their graves. Jesus was, after all, more than a prophet. He was and is the only begotten Son of God, and this resurrection miracle acts as a token or sign pointing to the final resurrection that will come at the end of the age when Jesus returns.

This then is the ninth and final miracle of Jesus that reflects a direct parallel miracle from the life and ministry of Elisha. It is a miracle that is found exclusively in Matthew's Gospel. It is recorded there because Matthew was painting a portrait of Jesus for a Jewish audience. For the perceptive, it is a portrait of a prophet who came in the miracle-working power of Elisha. And like any great storyteller, Matthew saved the most power-packed event until the end.

Will you and I be sparking a revival after our death as Elisha did?

7

A CALL FOR THE MIRACULOUS

*And these signs will accompany
those who believe:
In my name they will drive out demons;
they will speak in new tongues;
they will pick up snakes with their hands;
and when they drink deadly poison,
it will not hurt them at all;
they will place their hands on sick people,
and they will get well.*
(Mark 16:17–18)

What will it take to turn this nation and the world to faith in Jesus Christ? That question should set us on a Holy Spirit-driven quest to see a world-changing, book-of-Acts revival take place in our time.

There are those within the church who argue the age of miracles ended with the death of the original apostles. But those who hold such a view are not being true to the Scriptures, or the historical record of the church down through the ages.

Have you noticed that most revivals in the last hundred years involved a renewed emphasis on healing ministry? Many denominations have functionally delegated the healing ministry to the wastebin of New Testament history. "Sorry," they might say, "this is the wrong dispensation to get healed. Jesus does not do that anymore. Spiritual gifts like prophecy, tongues, and healing have all ceased since the publishing of the New Testament. If you are sick, all that is left is to go to your medical doctor and hope for the best." "If it be your will" prayers have become the dominant way of praying for the sick. Perhaps God wants us sick rather than whole nowadays.

Aimee Semple McPherson and A.B. Simpson, both Ontario-raised Canadians, were two people who challenged that assumption. Both asserted that spiritual gifts are still available today, including the gifts of healing. While both valued the role of medical doctors, they helped many discover that Jesus Christ our healer is the same yesterday, today, and forever (Hebrews 13:8). Both asserted that this is *not* the wrong dispensation to get healed by Jesus. He is still willing and able to heal the sick in body, mind, and spirit.

Both Semple McPherson and Simpson helped people rediscover the prayer of faith in James 5:14–15, where we read that if anyone is sick, they are to call the elders who will lay hands on them, anoint them with oil, and heal the sick by exercising the prayer of faith. They will be restored to health. By confessing their sins (like rage, unforgiveness, bitterness, and self-hatred) and praying for each other, many were healed. In the healing revival, it was noticed that people were often healed first spiritually and emotionally. The outer physical healings often naturally followed the inner healings.

Albert Benjamin Simpson was born on Prince Edward Island on December 15th, 1843, of Scottish Covenanter heritage. His family had emigrated from Morayshire, Scotland to Bayview, P.E.I. After the collapse of his father's shipbuilding business in the depression of the 1840s, his family moved from P.E.I. to a farm in western Ontario.

Fresh out of seminary in 1865, Simpson had accepted the call to pastor Knox Church in Hamilton, a congregation with the second largest Presbyterian church building in Canada. Over the next eight years, 750 new people joined the congregation.

Although he experienced success in his ministry, A.B. Simpson had become such a workaholic that he destroyed his health. In 1881, his medical doctor gave him just three months to live. But upon meeting an Episcopalian (Anglican) physician, Dr. Charles Cullis, at Old Orchard Camp in Maine, he experienced a remarkable healing of his near-fatal heart condition. His restoration to health was so complete that the next day, Simpson was able to climb a 3,000-foot mountain, and then successfully pray for his daughter Margaret's healing from diphtheria. This was the very disease which had earlier killed his son Melville.

Simpson believed that Jesus Christ is still healing people today (Hebrew 13:8). His first of many books was fittingly called *The Gospel of Healing*.

Word spread fast regarding these healings. He was inundated by many pleas for help. Others vilified and ridiculed him as another quack miracle worker. Simpson started Friday afternoon healing and holiness meetings, which quickly became New York City's most highly attended spiritual weekday meeting, with five hundred to one thousand in attendance. He even turned his own house into a healing home where people could come for prayer ministry.

Simpson, as founder of the Christian & Missionary Alliance, brought together four separate movements into one:

(1) missions and evangelism, (2) healing, (3) holiness, and (4) Jesus' Second Coming. His four-fold gospel emphasized "Christ our Savior, Sanctifier, Healer and Coming King." Simpson saw the healing ministry as vital in the fulfillment of the Great Commission to make disciples of all nations.

Few people nowadays realize that Aimee Semple McPherson was the most famous North American woman in the1920s. How is it a Canadian farm girl came to have a lasting impact on the lives of millions around the world?

Growing up on a farm near Salford, Ontario, Aimee Kennedy was raised in the Salvation Army by her mother.

At age seventeen, Aimee said, "Lord, I'll never eat or sleep again until you fill me with the Spirit of power."[1]

Having been touched by the Spirit, she married the visiting evangelist, Robert Semple. They promptly went to China as missionaries. But within months of their arrival in Hong Kong, her husband died after they both contracted malaria. Aimee came back to North America in 1912 as a broken woman, a widow, and a single mother of a daughter from her brief marriage.

She wrote: "I had come home from China like a wounded little bird, and my bleeding heart was constantly pierced with curious questions from well-meaning people."[2]

Remarrying on the rebound to the practical Harold McPherson, she tried unsuccessfully to be the traditional stay-at-home housewife her new husband wanted. It almost killed her. After ending up in hospital, and near death, God told her to go back to preaching. She said yes to her calling and was instantly healed.

---

[1] Daniel Mark Epstein, *Sister Aimee: The Life of Aimee Semple McPherson* (Harcourt Brace & Co, 1993), 52.

[2] Aimee Semple McPherson, "The Story of My Life," *Foursquare Crusader,* September 7, 1927, page 6.

Leaving that night with her two children, she began preaching in Canada. At her first meetings, only two men and a boy turned up for the first four days. Then, after miraculous healings broke out, the curious crowds appeared.

"My healings?" said Aimee. "I do nothing. If the eyes of the people are on me, nothing will happen. I pray and believe with others, who pray and believe, and the power of Christ works the miracle."[3]

The next step was travel to the West Coast. Aimee and her mom, Minnie Kennedy, became the first women to drive alone across North America on uncharted roads. After relocating to Los Angeles, Aimee became as well-known as Charlie Chaplin, Harry Houdini, and even President Teddy Roosevelt.

In the 1920s, the sheer number of medically verified healings at her services was astounding. This included the wheelchair-bound walking, the blind seeing, the deaf hearing, and tumors disappearing.

On January 1, 1923, Aimee Semple McPherson opened her headquarters church in Los Angeles, the 5,300 seat Angeles Temple. A typical Sunday would see Aimee preaching three services to a full house, while tens of thousands more listened on radio. Her influence on the culture of southern California was so profound that linguists attribute the present-day southern California accent to the impact she had on the language. In those formative years, so many heard her voice in person and via radio that she shaped the pronunciation and syntax of the daily speech of that region.

One month after opening Angeles Temple, Aimee started L.I.F.E. Bible College, which soon attracted 1,000 students. Many of those students became Foursquare pastors and missionaries who spread the Foursquare Gospel around the globe.

---

[3] Ibid.

Like AB Simpson, Aimee proclaimed a fourfold gospel message centered on Jesus—Jesus as Savior, Healer, Baptizer with the Holy Spirit, and Coming King. She called this the Foursquare Gospel and founded the denomination by that name.

Her legacy remains and flourishes. Today, there are 44,000 Foursquare Gospel churches in 143 countries around the world, and through the ministry of those churches, a million new believers committed their lives to Christ in the last calendar year.

But as we know, each new generation needs to discover the scope and power of the gospel for themselves. We cannot live on our parents' faith. We must experience God's grace firsthand. Undoubtedly, it was for this reason that Jude begins his epistle with these words:

> Dear friends, although I was very eager to write to you
> about the salvation we share, I felt compelled to write
> and urge you to contend for the faith that was once for
> all entrusted to God's holy people. (Jude 1:3)

Are we contending for the faith that was entrusted to us by the apostles? It is a faith that moved mountains of doubt, fear, and disability, and cast them into the sea. It is a faith that healed the sick, restored the crippled, and raised the widow Tabitha from her deathbed.[4] Are we contending for that kind of world-shaking, bondage-breaking faith?

The following testimony from evangelist R. W. Shambach illustrates the power of supernatural healing in bringing the lost to faith in Christ. Shambach made his first trip to India in 1956. He was gripped by the poverty and misery he saw in the

---

[4] Acts 28:8–9, Acts 3:1–10, Acts 9:32–43

marketplaces, and by the many he saw who were sick, crippled, and blind.

On that opening day, I preached for two hours, and my interpreter translated for two hours—for a total of four hours. They wanted me to go on. When I gave the altar call, I was so disappointed. I had preached to 50,000 people, and not one soul had come to accept Jesus.

Although no one came forward to accept Christ, and the crowd was obviously ready for the benediction, I said, "I am not done now. God says that signs follow His Word. I did what God called me to do. Now I am going to let God do what He said He was going to do."

I invited three people from the audience to come forward—they were beggars. I knew who they were. One was blind, one was deaf and dumb, and the other was a crippled woman who had never walked upright.

Fifty thousand people were watching.

They were all healed.

Do you know what happened? The people in that crowd started jumping out of trees, and a mob came running towards me… I never saw such an onslaught of people. They were yelling something at the top of their voice. I asked my interpreter, "What are they saying?"

He said, "They are hollering, 'Jesus is alive. Jesus is the Christ. Jesus is God.' They are coming to get saved."

What a thrill! Not one of them came when I preached, but when they saw the demonstration of the Gospel, they came.

God has called the Church to demonstrate His power.

Aren't you glad He is alive today?[5]

What will it take to turn this nation and the world to faith in Jesus Christ? Many are blind and hostile to God and the message of the gospel. The only thing that will open their eyes to the reality of Christ's love is a demonstration of the Lord's supernatural healing power.

Paul knew the importance of the miraculous in his ministry to the lost of his time.

> I came to you in weakness with great fear and trembling. My message and my preaching were not with wise and persuasive words, but with a demonstration of the Spirit's power, so that your faith might not rest on human wisdom, but on God's power. (1 Corinthians 2:3–5)

Is the gospel message we are presenting just wise and persuasive words? To be truly biblical, our message needs to be rooted in a demonstration of the Spirit's power.

Healing and the miraculous are an integral part of the Elisha Code. Let's not miss out on this key to future revivals.

---

[5] Excerpt From "Miracles: Eyewitness to the Miraculous" by R. W. Schambach, 2011. Kindle edition.

8

HE WHO IS LEAST

On that day you, Jerusalem,
will not be put to shame
for all the wrongs you have done to me,
because I will remove from you
your arrogant boasters.
Never again will you be haughty
on my holy hill.
But I will leave within you the meek
and humble.
The remnant of Israel will trust in the
name of the LORD.
(Zephaniah 3:11–12)

The previous chapter concluded with Paul declaring he came to the Corinthians *"in weakness with great fear and trembling"* (1 Corinthians 2:3), but despite his weakness, God mightily used him to demonstrate the Spirit's power.

There is something quite contradictory or paradoxical about Paul's statement in 1 Corinthians 2:3–5, but this paradox of strength in weakness follows a consistent pattern in

Paul's epistles. He begins his first letter to the Corinthians by highlighting one of these apparent contradictions.

> Brothers and sisters, think of what you were when you were called. Not many of you were wise by human standards; not many were influential; not many were of noble birth. But God chose the foolish things of the world to shame the wise; God chose the weak things of the world to shame the strong. God chose the lowly things of this world and the despised things—and the things that are not—to nullify the things that are, so that no one may boast before him. (1 Corinthians 1:26–29)

Paul is telling us that God and his kingdom operate on entirely different principles than the values and philosophies of this world. God uses and shows favor to those who are weak, foolish, and of low status in the eyes of the world. God's kingdom is a totally upside-down kingdom according to the world's perspective.

Paul elaborates further on the contradictory, paradoxical nature of God's kingdom in his second letter to the Corinthians when he states, *"That is why, for Christ's sake, I delight in weaknesses, in insults, in hardships, in persecutions, in difficulties. For when I am weak, then I am strong"* (2 Corinthians 12:10).

This call for humility and submission is not confined to Paul's letters. Peter explicitly calls for the same.

> All of you, clothe yourselves with humility toward one another, because,
>
> > "God opposes the proud but shows favor to the humble."

Humble yourselves, therefore, under God's mighty hand, that he may lift you up in due time. (1 Peter 5:5b–6)

James repeats this call for humility in his epistle. In fact, in their appeal James and Peter quote the same verse, Proverbs 3:34. (See James 4:6–7.)

The apostles' teaching and lived experience simply reflected the teaching of their Lord and master Jesus Christ. Jesus' life was a continual paradox. He was born in a stable, yet his birth was heralded by angels, the appearance of a star, and the arrival of magi from foreign lands. Then, he began his ministry with a manifesto that sets the operating principles of our world on its head.

Blessed are the poor in spirit,
> for theirs is the kingdom of heaven.
> Blessed are those who mourn,
> for they will be comforted.
> Blessed are the meek,
> for they will inherit the earth.
> Blessed are those who hunger
> and thirst for righteousness,
> for they will be filled.
> Blessed are the merciful,
> for they will be shown mercy.
> Blessed are the pure in heart,
> for they will see God.
> Blessed are the peacemakers,
> for they will be called children of God.
> Blessed are those who are persecuted
> because of righteousness,

for theirs is the kingdom of heaven.
(Matthew 5:3–10)

Jesus' ministry centered on the poor, the sick, the oppressed, and the afflicted. Peter described Jesus' life work with these words, *"…God anointed Jesus of Nazareth with the Holy Spirit and power, and… he went around doing good and healing all who were under the power of the devil, because God was with him"* (Acts 10:38).

Jesus was the eternal Creator of all things, yet through the miracle of incarnation, he willingly subjected himself to the frailties and limitations of humanity. That included the humiliation of suffering the death of a criminal on a cruel Roman cross.

This upside-down perspective is at the heart of the Elisha Code as revealed in the eleventh chapter of Matthew. In the previous chapters of this book, we recounted how the miracles of Jesus run parallel to the miracles of the prophet Elisha. In fact, there is a striking similarity in the content, style, and tenor of the ministries of Jesus and Elisha.

Furthermore, in Matthew eleven, Jesus definitively states that John the Baptist *"is the Elijah who is to come"* (Matthew 11:14, CSB). Again, there is a remarkable similarity in the intent, tone, and scope of the ministries of John and Elijah. So then, chapter eleven of Matthew establishes the link between the Old Testament prophetic duo of Elijah and Elisha and the New Testament duo of John the Baptist and Jesus Christ.

But in his description of John, Jesus goes on to make a statement that is rather puzzling and frequently misunderstood or misinterpreted.

Truly I tell you, among those born of women there has not risen anyone greater than John the Baptist; yet whoever is least in the kingdom of heaven is greater than he. (Matthew 11:11)

The first part of this statement is very straightforward, though quite startling. Clearly, Jesus held John in the highest regard—higher than any human past or present. Higher than Abraham. Higher than Moses. Higher than David. Higher than any of the Old Testament prophets. Jesus places John the Baptist at the head of the list, above all who ever lived. That is quite the honor!

But then Jesus goes on to say, *"yet whoever is least in the kingdom of heaven is greater than he."*

So, who then is greater than John?

Evangelicals have puzzled over the meaning of this statement. Some have come up with a rather elaborate interpretation that relies heavily on dispensational theology. They reason that John was not born again; therefore, he is not included in the kingdom of heaven. Hence, anyone who is born again under the New Testament dispensation is greater than John.

However, this dispensational interpretation runs into several obstacles when we compare it with the whole of Scripture.

First, let's be unequivocally clear. Spiritual rebirth is essential to anyone's entrance into the kingdom of God. Jesus said, *"Most assuredly, I say to you, unless one is born again, he cannot see the kingdom of God"* (John 3:3, NKJV). We must come into relationship with God—be born into his kingdom to be citizens of the kingdom.

Jesus' statement in John 3:3 raises other questions concerning the believers of the Old Testament era. Will we see them in heaven? Are they citizens of the kingdom?

There is ample biblical evidence that John the Baptist and all the great saints of the Old Testament are citizens of the kingdom. In fact, in Luke's Gospel, Jesus said just that.

> There will be weeping and gnashing of teeth, when you see Abraham and Isaac and Jacob and all the prophets in the kingdom of God, and yourselves thrust out. They will come from the east and the west, from the north and the south, and sit down in the kingdom of God. And indeed there are last who will be first, and there are first who will be last. (Luke 13:28–30, NKJV)

Moreover, in Matthew 11, Jesus identifies John as being greater than all the prophets.

> Then what did you go out to see? A prophet? Yes, I tell you, and more than a prophet. This is the one about whom it is written: "I will send my messenger ahead of you, who will prepare your way before you." (Matthew 11:9–10)

If the patriarchs and prophets of the old covenant are included in the kingdom of God, then surely John, whom Jesus identifies as being greater than them all, is included as well.

Furthermore, Hebrews 11 makes it abundantly clear that great Old Testament heroes of the faith will be present with us in glory. In fact, they are part of a great cloud of witnesses cheering us on (Hebrews 12:1–3).

So from these scriptures it is clear that the Old Testament heroes of the faith are all citizens of the kingdom. But Jesus said they cannot be citizens of the kingdom unless they are born again (John 3:3). How can they be born again when that teaching had not been introduced yet? In John 3, Jesus provides the answer to that conundrum.

> The wind blows where it wishes, and you hear the sound of it, but cannot tell where it comes from and

where it goes. So is everyone who is born of the Spirit. (John 3:8, NKJV)

Rebirth happens by the Spirit, and it has been happening from the very beginning. The day may come when we will meet with Enoch, Moses, and David in the kingdom.

The wind of the Spirit was blowing in the hearts of John the Baptist and the Old Testament citizens of the spiritual kingdom, and they were born again by the Spirit. This must be so, or Jesus could not say what he said in Luke 13:28–30 where he identifies them as sitting down in the kingdom of God. (They could not be sitting down in the kingdom of God unless they were born again.)

Moreover, there are not two kingdoms of God, one for the Old Testament believers and one for the New Testament born-again believers. There is only one eternal, spiritual kingdom of God, and we will all sit together in it.

Jesus is, after all, the great unifier of Jews and Gentiles—just as Paul states.

In reading this, then, you will be able to understand my insight into the mystery of Christ, which was not made known to people in other generations as it has now been revealed by the Spirit to God's holy apostles and prophets. This mystery is that through the gospel the Gentiles are heirs together with Israel, members together of one body, and sharers together in the promise in Christ Jesus. (Ephesians 3:4–6)

Jesus introduced us to the understanding of being born again, but that does not mean spiritual rebirth was not happening before he introduced that teaching. Isaac Newton introduced us to the concept of gravity, but that does not mean the laws of gravity were not working until he introduced them.

Similarly, Dr. Frederick Banting and Dr. Charles Best discovered insulin in 1921, and in January 1922 they injected insulin into a dying fourteen-year-old type one diabetic named Leonard Thompson. The transformation in Leonard's body was nothing short of miraculous. Until that time, a diagnosis of type one diabetes was viewed as a death sentence. Most patients died within weeks or months.

We too, like Leonard Thompson, are under a death sentence. We suffer from a deadly condition called a sinful nature. The cure for this condition is spiritual rebirth at the hands of the Great Physician, Jesus Christ.

Insulin was doing its life-sustaining work in human bodies long before Banting and Best discovered it. In the same way, the Spirit was at work drawing people like Moses and David into relationship with the heavenly Father long before Jesus had his conversation with Nicodemus in John 3. And Old Testament people like Deborah, Ruth, Esther, and Jeremiah responded in faith as the Spirit of God touched their lives. They too came into a life-altering relationship with God—a relationship that we now call being born again.

Logic dictates that these Old Testament saints must have experienced rebirth, or they could not sit down in the kingdom of God as Jesus declares they will in Luke 13:28–30.

Consequently, Jesus' statement in Matthew 11:11 about *"whoever is least in the kingdom of God"* is not about setting up a distinction between those who are born again, and those who are not born again, or drawing a distinction between the Old Testament and New Testament dispensations. Rather, it's a passage about humility, where Jesus takes on the identity of being the one who is least in the kingdom of God.

Now let's again look at Matthew 11:11 with fresh eyes.

> Truly I tell you, among those born of women there
> has not risen anyone greater than John the Baptist; yet
> whoever is least in the kingdom of heaven is greater
> than he. (Matthew 11:11)

After stating that John is the greatest man who ever lived,
Jesus asserts that the one who is least in the kingdom is greater
than John.

So, who is greater than John?

Surely, we can all agree that Jesus is greater than John. He
is, after all, the king of the kingdom. But in true contradictory,
paradoxical fashion Jesus casts himself as being least in the
kingdom of God. Jesus takes on that identity because he came
to serve, suffer, and die.

So then, Matthew 11:11 is a passage that portrays Jesus
humbling himself and taking the lowest position, although he is
King of all. This is the ultimate paradox expressed in a brilliant
turn of phrase—so brilliant its meaning has eluded more than
a few theologians.

Paul beautifully describes Christ's humiliation and
subsequent exaltation with these familiar words:

> Who, being in very nature God,
>> did not consider equality with God something to
>> be used to his own advantage;
>> rather, he made himself nothing
>> by taking the very nature of a servant,
>> being made in human likeness.
>> And being found in appearance as a man,
>> he humbled himself

> by becoming obedient to death—
> even death on a cross!
> Therefore God exalted him to the highest place
> and gave him the name that is above every name,
> that at the name of Jesus every knee should bow,
> in heaven and on earth and under the earth,
> and every tongue acknowledge
> that Jesus Christ is Lord,
> to the glory of God the Father. (Philippians 2:6–11)

With his statement in Matthew 11:11, Jesus is making himself nothing and taking on the very nature of a servant just as Paul describes.

Furthermore, this self-deprecation follows a pattern that we see repeated in Matthew's Gospel. Jesus repeatedly tells reverse stories, paradoxical parables where the first will be last. (See Matthew 18:1–5, Matthew 19:30, Matthew 20:16, and Matthew 20:28.) These passages assert that Jesus and his kingdom work on principles and values that are the opposite of those found in the world. The poor have true wealth. The weak are strong. The despised are honored. Matthew 11:11 fits into this pattern of reversal, with Jesus taking the lowest or least position.

But why is this emphasis on humility significant? What is the application for us today? Humility is at the core of the Elisha Code. We too need to follow in the footsteps of Jesus. We too need to humble ourselves and serve as he did.

The world will not be won to Christ by millionaire evangelists and pastors crisscrossing the globe in their private jets and preaching a gospel of prosperity and self-fulfillment. The world will be won by the meek—those who know how to humble themselves and serve, serve at the cost of their lives as the first-century apostles did. That is the Jesus way—the way of the cross.

9

THE SERVANT OF ALL

Sitting down, Jesus called the Twelve and said,
"Anyone who wants to be first must be the very
last, and the servant of all."
(Mark 9:35)

Are you and I putting Jesus' teaching on being the least into practice in our daily lives? Are we becoming the servant of all? Do we see ourselves as last or do we put ourselves and our concerns first above all others?

Why is humility so key to missionary breakthrough? In what way has pride and self-righteousness either prevented or killed times of revival? The beloved devotional writer Andrew Murray has much to teach us in these key areas.

Andrew's father, Andrew Senior, had come to South Africa from Scotland as a missionary in 1828. The Dutch Reformed Church was so desperate for pastors that they would even accept Scottish Presbyterians into their fold. Revival and missions were the air that Andrew Junior breathed in his father's house. Missionaries constantly visited the Murray home, including Dr. David Livingstone.

In 1838, when Andrew Junior was ten, he and his brother John were sent by their parents to study in Scotland. In the spring of 1840, the revivalist William C. Burns came and spoke in Aberdeen, Scotland. Burns' heart was constantly broken over the lost, and he would weep and pray for hours for their salvation. This left a deep impression on young Andrew Murray.

The two brothers then went to Utrecht, Holland, for further theological studies. There, they became part of a revival group called *Sechor Dabar* ("remember the Word" in Hebrew).

When he returned to South Africa, Andrew became a Dutch Reformed pastor, being elected six times as the Moderator of the entire Dutch Reformed Church denomination. After initially trying to shut down the 1860 South African revival, he ended up giving strong leadership to this key revival. As people cried out in anguish, Andrew initially said, "This must stop now. I am your pastor!" God changed his mind, so, with Andrew's blessing, great renewal broke out throughout South Africa with many thousands confessing Christ.

Suddenly in 1879, at age fifty-one, Murray lost his voice for two years. Out of his painful time of silence, he learned to depend upon God's faithfulness, surrendering everything to God, and coming into a deep place of humility and love for others. In this time of waiting, he learned that we have nothing but what we humbly receive from God. Humility is about being an empty vessel that God can fill. Are we willing to be radically dependent on God?

Andrew's amazing book *Humility* came out of this deep time of self-crucifixion. He wrote, "Nothing but a crucified Jesus revealed in the soul can give a humble spirit."[1]

Humility for Andrew was most clearly seen in the incarnate and crucified Christ who prayed "not my will but Thine be

[1] Lena Choy. *Andrew Murray: The Authorized Biography.* CLC Publications. Kindle Edition, Location 1323.

done." Andrew discovered that "pride is death, and the other (humility) is life; the one is all hell, the other is all heaven."[2]

During his voice ailment, Andrew came to see that a lack of humility suppresses revival and missions. He wrote, "A lack of humility is the explanation of every defect and failure."[3]

In 1881, he went to London to Bethshan, a healing home started by W. E. Boardman. He was completely healed there and never had trouble with his voice again. From that point on, he knew and taught that spiritual gifts are for believers today, and that God's will is for healing and wholeness. While in England in 1882, he attended the Keswick Convention, which focused on holiness and deeper life in Christ. Eventually, he founded Keswick South Africa.

Andrew did not just recover his voice; his whole demeanor changed. He became known for his joyful humour. A long-time friend of the family wrote to Murray's daughter Mary of this transformation: "A great change came into his life after that. He used to be rather stern and very decided in his judgment of things—after that year he was all love. His great humility also struck me very forcibly at that time."[4]

Murray's oldest daughter agreed, saying, "He began to show in all relationships constant tenderness and unruffled lovingkindness and unselfish thought for others which increasingly characterized his life from that point."[5]

God showed Andrew Murray that "manifestations of temper and touchiness and irritation, feelings of bitterness

---

[2] Ibid.

[3] Andrew Murray, *Humility: The Journey toward Holiness,* 1895. Available at https://www.goodreads.com/quotes/539647-humility-is-the-only-soil-in-which-the-graces-root, accessed August 23, 2023.

[4] Vance Christie, *Andrew Murray: Christ's Anointed Minister to South Africa.* Christian Focus Publications. Kindle edition, 208.

[5] Ibid, 214.

and estrangement, have their root in nothing but pride." [6] He concluded that our defensiveness and unkind words reveal a lack of humility.

This deep personal change is the hallmark of all who come to a point of full repentance and faith in Christ. Humility is the mark of those who have been broken by the Spirit.

In his play *The Power of Darkness,* Leo Tolstoy put these words in the mouth of one of the main characters, "Everyone thinks of changing the world, but no one thinks of changing himself."[7]

World-changers—God's world-changers—have first been changed by the Spirit of God. The self has been crucified and now Christ reigns. Leo Tolstoy, Andrew Murray, and the apostle Paul knew they were in desperate need of personal transformation. Real change begins with humble submission to Christ, the crucified Lord and Savior.

> I have been crucified with Christ and I no longer live,
> but Christ lives in me. The life I now live in the body, I
> live by faith in the Son of God, who loved me and gave
> himself for me. (Galatians 2:20)

Andrew Murray ended up writing two hundred and forty books and booklets, including *Waiting on God, The School of Obedience, Absolute Surrender,* and *The Deeper Christian Life.* His anointed pen came from his anointed heart.

One of his most transformative books was called *The Key to the Missionary Problem,* in which he taught that missions were "the chief end of the church." Dr. F.B. Meyer said that *The Key*

---

[6] Lena Choy, *Andrew Murray: The Authorized Biography.* CLC Publications. Kindle Edition, 1323.

[7] Leo Tolstoy, *The Power of Darkness.* Kindle edition, 2012. Aylmer Maude & Louise Shanks Maude, translators.

to the Missionary Problem, if widely read, would lead to one of the greatest revivals of missionary enthusiasm that the world has ever known.

Andrew Murray saw missions as so large and difficult that they required the Church to return to "the Pentecostal life of her first love."

"The Pentecostal commission can only be carried out by a Pentecostal Church in Pentecostal Power… We have given too much attention to methods and to machinery and to resources and too little to the Source of Power—the filling with the Holy Ghost."[8]

Humble prayer, said Murray, was the heart of missions. He prayed that the cry of our whole heart, night, and day, would be, "Oh, for the humility of Jesus in myself and all around me!"[9]

Murray saw humility as an essential key to winning the lost, reflecting the true character of Jesus. Oh, that God would use such humility to breathe a revival of missions throughout the world!

God eventually used Andrew as a peacemaker, humbly seeking to avoid the horrendous Boer/Anglo War (October 11, 1899–May 31, 1902), during which 26,000 of the 100,000 women and children in British concentration camps died of malnutrition and disease. Andrew Murray was ideally suited to the task of peacemaking. He had spent his entire working life as a bridge builder between the Dutch-speaking Afrikaners and the black tribal communities. Now, as a British-born church leader, he interceded for peace in the face of British imperial aggression.

---

[8] Vance Christie, *Andrew Murray: Christ's Anointed Minister to South Africa*. Christian Focus Publications. Kindle Edition, 269.

[9] J. Du Plessis, *Andrew Murray of South Africa* (London: Marshall Brothers Limited, 1919), 440.

He wrote, "The horrors of war are too terrible; the sin and shame of war are too great; the folly of war is too monstrous... I believe with my whole heart that in many respects Britain is the noblest, the most Christian nation in the world, its greatest power for good or evil... Once again, I beseech the Christian people of Great Britain to rouse themselves, and to say, 'This war shall not be.' Let every lover of peace make his voice heard."[10]

In this time of tragic conflict, in various hot spots around the globe, we should pray that other humble peacemakers, like Andrew Murray, may arise. What might it take for the Russian and Ukrainian people to humbly seek lasting reconciliation and forgiveness?

The earnest prayer and humility of Jesus points the way forward. The hour is late. Hear our Savior's plea, *"Couldn't you men keep watch with me for one hour?"* (Matthew 26:40).

---

[10] Vance Christie, *Andrew Murray: Christ's Anointed Minister to South Africa*. Christian Focus Publications. Kindle Edition, 269.

10

REGIME CHANGE:
THE MISSION OF THE DYNAMIC DUO

At that time Jesus, full of joy
through the Holy Spirit, said,
"I praise you, Father, Lord of heaven and earth,
because you have hidden these things from the
wise and learned,
and revealed them to little children.
Yes, Father, for this is what you were
pleased to do."
(Luke 10:21)

Before sunrise on February 24, 2022, Russia launched a multi-pronged attack on Ukraine by air, land, and sea. Kyiv, the capital, was expected to fall within days. President Biden offered to evacuate Ukrainian President Volodymyr Zelenskyy from the besieged capital. But a resolute and defiant Zelensky replied, "I need ammunition, not a ride."[1]

---

[1] "Volodymyr Zelenskiy stands defiant in face of Russian attack," *The Guardian*, 26 February 2022. Retrieved 2 March 2022.

What was Vladimir Putin's objective in launching this unprovoked Russian attack on his smaller southern neighbor? His immediate goal was regime change. He wanted to oust the democratic, pro-western government of Ukraine and replace it with a pro-Russian regime subservient to his will.

Putin failed in his immediate objective. The Ukrainian defenders mounted a fierce resistance. The invaders were beaten back, though they engaged in rape and wanton killing of civilians, and inflicted massive destruction.

At the time of this writing, the war rages on. The outcome remains uncertain. Regime change may yet come. But will the regime change be in Kyiv or in Moscow? Time will tell.

Here is what we know with certainty from the Scriptures. The LORD wants regime change.

Elijah and Elisha, the Old Testament dynamic duo, were on a mission. They had an assignment directly from the LORD God Almighty. What was their mission—the task the LORD had assigned to them?

In broad terms their assignment was regime change. The northern Kingdom of Israel had turned its back on God—the God who generations earlier had rescued them from slavery in Egypt. Worse yet, Israel had turned to idolatry. Under the autocratic rule of Ahab and Jezebel, the worship of the fertility gods Baal and Asherah flourished.[2]

First Elijah, and then Elisha, was tasked with bringing the wayward people of God back to worshipping Yahweh. But King Ahab and Queen Jezebel—Satan's power couple—stood in the way.

---

[2] "'I have not made trouble for Israel,' Elijah replied. 'But you and your father's family have. You have abandoned the LORD's commands and have followed the Baals. Now summon the people from all over Israel to meet me on Mount Carmel. And bring the four hundred and fifty prophets of Baal and the four hundred prophets of Asherah, who eat at Jezebel's table'" (1 Kings 18:18–20).

Above all, this was a life and death struggle for the minds and hearts of the people.

Amid a famine brought on by a severe drought, some dared to defy Israel's king and queen. Obadiah, Ahab's palace administrator, was such a man. A devout believer in the LORD, Obadiah risked his life.

> While Jezebel was killing off the LORD's prophets, Obadiah had taken a hundred prophets and hidden them in two caves, fifty in each, and had supplied them with food and water. (1 Kings 18:4)

In response, Elijah courageously confronted King Ahab and challenged him to assemble all of Israel for a duel to the death on Mount Carmel. Ahab was to bring with him *"the four hundred and fifty prophets of Baal and the four hundred prophets of Asherah, who eat at Jezebel's table"* (1 Kings 18:19).

Thus the stage was set for what many consider the greatest challenge and display of God's power in the Hebrew Scriptures.

> Elijah went before the people and said, "How long will you waver between two opinions? If the LORD is God, follow him; but if Baal is God, follow him."
>
> But the people said nothing.
>
> Then Elijah said to them, "I am the only one of the LORD's prophets left, but Baal has four hundred and fifty prophets. Get two bulls for us. Let Baal's prophets choose one for themselves, and let them cut it into pieces and put it on the wood but not set fire to it. I will prepare the other bull and put it on the wood but not set fire to it. Then you call on the name of your god, and I will call on the name of the LORD. The god who answers by fire—he is God."

THE ELISHA CODE & THE COMING REVIVAL

Then all the people said, "What you say is good."
(1 Kings 18:21–24)

The LORD vindicated his prophet, Elijah, by sending fire
from heaven that *"burned up the sacrifice, the wood, the stones
and the soil, and also licked up the water in the trench"* (1 Kings
18:38).

The prophets of Baal were vanquished.[3] But rather than
turning on Ahab and having him killed as well, Elijah declared
the king should go and celebrate because a drought-ending
rainfall was on its way. Then Elijah ascended the mountain, fell
on his knees, and prayed for the rain to come, and after much
prayer the downpour arrives.[4]

Why this show of mercy to Ahab, the tyrant and accessory
to murder?[5] If the ultimate goal was regime change, then why
not eliminate the man who stood in the way? Why didn't the
prophet mete out God's wrath and retribution? Instead, Elijah
portrayed mercy and the abundant grace of God. Why?

The answer lies at the heart of the gospel message, which,
according to Jesus, is all about regime change. It's about letting
King Jesus rule our hearts and minds. The government that
affects us most directly isn't in Washington, London, Moscow,
or Ottawa, and it isn't in a state or provincial capital. The
government that affects us most directly is the government of
our heart and mind. Is Jesus enthroned there? Is he governing
your decision making? Is he calling the shots?

Far too often, we think a change of government at the
national, state, or local level will transform our lives. That's a

---

[3] "Then Elijah commanded them, 'Seize the prophets of Baal. Don't let anyone
get away!' They seized them, and Elijah had them brought down to the Kishon
Valley and slaughtered there" (1 Kings 18:40).
[4] 1 Kings 18:41–45
[5] 1 Kings 18:4, 1 Kings 21:1–16

political fantasy politicians love to peddle. True transformational change begins at the individual level. And there is nothing more transformational than spiritual rebirth. Jesus' conversation with Nicodemus reveals that truth.[6]

In Elijah's interaction with Ahab, we see this principle of repentance and rebirth at work. Elijah was working to change the heart of the king. He wanted to see the LORD enthroned there. What could bring about that profound change in King Ahab's heart?

Clearly there was a need for repentance. And what could bring about that change? A jaw-dropping, heart-stopping demonstration of God's power set the stage for genuine repentance. Surely, the miracle of fire falling from heaven would result in a change of heart and a change in allegiance—a change from the worship of Baal to the worship of Yahweh.

Secondly, nothing melts stony hearts like the kindness and mercy of God. Elijah demonstrated that mercy by his treatment of Ahab, and by praying for the rain that ended a three-and-a-half-year drought and famine in the land.[7]

There is something extravagant about the patience and mercy of God.

Don't forget that the Lord is patient because he wants people to be saved. (2 Peter 3:15a, CEV)

Or do you show contempt for the riches of his kindness, forbearance and patience, not realizing that God's kindness is intended to lead you to repentance? (Romans 2:4)

---

[6] John 3:1–21
[7] James 5:17–18

In his interactions with Ahab, Elijah consistently displayed the undeserved kindness and patience of God. Nothing demonstrates this better than Elijah's confrontation of Ahab after the incident involving Naboth's vineyard. Jezebel plotted to have Naboth killed, and Ahab then seized Naboth's land.[8]

Elijah spoke these prophetic words to the king:

This is what the LORD says: In the place where dogs licked up Naboth's blood, dogs will lick up your blood—yes, yours! (1 Kings 21:19)

Of Jezebel, Elijah said:

And also concerning Jezebel the LORD says: "Dogs will devour Jezebel by the wall of Jezreel." (1 Kings 21:23)

But what happened next is truly astonishing. We read that Ahab *"tore his clothes, put on sackcloth and fasted. He lay in sackcloth and went around meekly"* (1 Kings 21:27).

And how did the LORD respond to Ahab's apparent repentance and contrition?

Then the word of the Lord came to Elijah the Tishbite: "Have you noticed how Ahab has humbled himself before me? Because he has humbled himself, I will not bring this disaster in his day, but I will bring it on his house in the days of his son." (1 Kings 21:28–29)

What this turn of events demonstrates is the power of personal repentance. Genuine repentance has the power to

---

[8] 1 Kings 21:1–16

change the course of history. It prevented the brutal end to Ahab's dynasty during his lifetime.

Was Ahab's repentance genuine? We can certainly debate that question. It appears that Ahab turned away from sin, but did he turn his affections to the Lord? Did he seek after God? Or was this a caught-with-a-hand-in-the-cookie-jar repentance that signaled he was sorry to be caught, but not sorry enough to change his ways?

Let's remember that true biblical repentance brings about a regime change in the mind. The selfish ego that ruled for so long must abdicate. God is in charge now. King Jesus governs our thoughts and actions.

Perhaps Ahab experienced a measure of true repentance, but the real power—the true ruler of his life—was Queen Jezebel. She suppressed Ahab's repentance and conversion, both after fire fell from heaven at Mount Carmel, and after Elijah confronted him over the incident involving Naboth's vineyard.

For national regime change to occur, the true power behind the throne needs to repent or be replaced. But in this case, the kingpin was not the king. The kingpin was Queen Jezebel. All of Elijah's efforts appear to be aimed at King Ahab. But the queen remained untouched, unchanged, and unrepentant. And she ruled the day.

By faith, Elijah engineered an astonishing display of God's power at Mount Carmel. But shortly thereafter, he also displayed an astonishing level of cowardice in the face of Jezebel's threats.

Frequently, a great victory is followed by great temptation.

Now Ahab told Jezebel everything Elijah had done and how he had killed all the prophets with the sword. So Jezebel sent a messenger to Elijah to say, "May the gods deal with me, be it ever so severely, if by this time tomorrow I do not make your life like that of one of them."

Elijah was afraid and ran for his life. (1 Kings 19:1–3)

How could this prophet display such raw courage one day, and on the next day wilt before the threats of this depraved woman? After all, Jezebel was calling on the same disgraced gods that Elijah had revealed as powerless a day earlier. Where was the God of Elijah now in the face of this threat? Was he hiding, or had he fallen asleep?

Of course not! But the prophet succumbed to his fleshly nature, sheer exhaustion, and the fear of man—or more precisely the fear of a woman.

Some psychologists see the classic hallmarks of a manic-depressive in Elijah's response. He swings from extreme highs to extreme lows. He storms the mountain heights of emotion, exerts himself to an extreme,[9] and then sinks into the depths of despair.

After fleeing to Horeb, the mountain of God, twice Elijah lays out his complaint before the LORD.

I have been very zealous for the LORD God Almighty. The Israelites have rejected your covenant, torn down your altars, and put your prophets to death with the sword. I am the only one left, and now they are trying to kill me too. (1 Kings 19:14)

How does the LORD respond to Elijah's complaint? He has him appoint his successor and then corrects his self-pitying exaggeration. The modern equivalent might be an

---

[9] 1 Kings 18:44–46

announcement from your boss that you are fired for just cause. Let's take a closer look at the LORD's reply to Elijah:

> Go back the way you came, and go to the Desert of Damascus. When you get there, anoint Hazael king over Aram. Also, anoint Jehu son of Nimshi king over Israel, and anoint Elisha son of Shaphat from Abel Meholah to succeed you as prophet. Jehu will put to death any who escape the sword of Hazael, and Elisha will put to death any who escape the sword of Jehu. Yet I reserve seven thousand in Israel—all whose knees have not bowed down to Baal and whose mouths have not kissed him. (1 Kings 19:15–18)

Let's first look at Elijah's lie and Yahweh's response to it. Yes, Elijah lied. He said he was the only prophet of the LORD left, yet Obadiah specifically told Elijah that as a faithful follower of the LORD since his youth, he had hidden a hundred prophets of the LORD in two caves.[10] Yet, before the people gathered on Mount Carmel, Elijah repeated his boast about being the only prophet of the LORD left in the land.[11] Clearly this was not true.

Furthermore, there was false humility in Elijah's plea before the LORD. He stated, *"I have been very zealous for the LORD God Almighty."* Though he had been zealous, he made his zeal a point of pride. He compared himself with others and concluded their faith and sacrifices in the face of severe persecution merited no consideration. To him, his efforts alone were noteworthy. Thus, he concluded he was the only faithful man left.

Depression begins when we believe a lie. Elijah believed the lie that he alone was faithful to Yahweh. In addition, depression

[10] 1 Kings 18:12–15
[11] 1 Kings 18:22

breeds isolation and self-pity. Both are hallmarks of the state Elijah was in.

Sadly, this great man of God fell short, and now a replacement was needed to continue the deep work he had set in motion in Israel. The will and purpose of God must prevail. But the LORD uses pure vessels rather than those tainted by pride.[12]

Elijah's failings all too frequently have been repeated by churches and ministries through the annals of history. God dramatically uses an individual or a movement to bring about a spiritual awakening or renewal. But then pride sets in. A sense of superiority emerges. This is coupled with a degree of exclusivity that manifests itself by restricting fellowship to a certain group or an inner circle. Attitudes or statements declaring that, "We alone have the full truth" begin to emerge.

Soon the Spirit that was so evidently present in the early days of fruitful ministry is absent. Pride sets in and the Holy Spirit flees. The LORD will use a different vessel—the humble vessel wiped clean.

There is a striking parallel between the ministry of Elijah and John the Baptist:

- There appears to be a very deliberate attempt by John to take on the appearance of Elijah in his dress, diet, and demeanor.[13]
- Both men boldly called the nation to repentance.
- Both directly confronted the political leaders of their time (Ahab and Herod Antipas).
- Both sank into states of depression and questioned their ministry (Elijah at Mount Horeb, John while imprisoned).
- Both had their life and ministry undermine or cut short by a woman (Jezebel and Herodias).

[12] 2 Timothy 2:19–21
[13] 2 Kings 1:8, Matthew 3:1–4

REGIME CHANGE: THE MISSION OF THE DYNAMIC DUO

- Both sought regime change but failed to see it in their day.
- Both sowed the seeds of a remarkable transition.
- Both were succeeded by men who brought the work they began to fruition (Elisha and Jesus).

With Elijah's fiery departure, the mission of regime change fell to Elisha to accomplish. A double portion of Elijah's anointing now rested on him, and under the LORD's guidance, through his ministry Elisha performed miracle after miracle—fourteen in total, doubling Elijah's total.

Though the overall mission of this prophetic dynamic duo remained the same, there are some striking differences between Elijah and Elisha in terms of their calling, ministry, character, and personality. In the same vein, there are striking differences between the New Testament duo of John the Baptist and Jesus.

First, we should note that Elisha came from a wealthy farm family. We read that at the time of his calling, he was plowing with twelve yoke of oxen. A common farm family might have a single yoke (pair) of oxen, but Elisha was plowing with twelve yoke (twenty-four oxen). That's an astonishing number, and it implies the family farm is enormous.

> Elijah went up to him and threw his cloak around him. Elisha then left his oxen and ran after Elijah. "Let me kiss my father and mother goodbye," he said, "and then I will come with you."
>
> "Go back," Elijah replied. "What have I done to you?"
>
> So Elisha left him and went back. He took his yoke of oxen and slaughtered them. He burned the plowing equipment to cook the meat and gave it to the people, and they ate. Then he set out to follow Elijah and became his servant. (1 Kings 19:19b–21)

Elisha left all to follow Elijah. There is something highly symbolic about Elisha's sacrifice of his oxen and the burning of his plow. In his farewell, he burned the bridges back to his former lifestyle. It's a stunning about-face for a wealthy young man. Elisha turned his back on the riches and prestige of this world to become the servant/slave of a homeless roving prophet.

Jesus, the prophet of the new covenant, left his throne in glory to become the servant of all. He set aside the wealth of heaven to serve among the poor. He asks his followers to do the same. Some, like Peter, James, John, and Matthew, the tax collector, heeded his call, left all, and followed him. Others, like the rich young ruler, clung to the security of their wealth.[14]

It's striking that Elijah repeatedly tried to dissuade Elisha from following him.[15] Yet, Elisha persisted. Similarly, Jesus repeatedly warned his followers of the cost they would bear in becoming his disciples.[16] Have you and I persevered in following Jesus despite hardship and opposition?

Second, Elisha was a man of the people, whereas Elijah was a man of solitude—a man of the desert wilderness.

Elijah spent months—possibly years—hidden in a ravine while he was fed by ravens.[17] Again when he fled from Jezebel, he first retreated to the wilderness and then went on a forty-day trek into the Sinai Desert and Horeb, the mountain of God.[18] Elijah chose long periods of isolation, and God spoke to him during these times.

By contrast, in the biblical record there are no extended periods in which Elisha self-isolated. Instead, we see a man who was actively engaged with others. His leadership role in the

[14] Matthew 19:16–24, Mark 10:17–23, Luke 18:18–30
[15] 1 Kings 19:20, 2 Kings 2:2, 2:4, 2:6
[16] Matthew 8:18–22, Luke 14:25–33, Matthew 10:37–39
[17] 1 Kings 17:1–9
[18] 1 Kings 19:3–9

company of the prophets illustrates his gregarious nature. He is portrayed as a man of food and fellowship.[19]

In his social life Elisha resembles Jesus, his New Testament counterpart. He too was outgoing—a man of the people. Similarly, Elijah, the austere prophet, resembles John the Baptist in his spartan ways and his desert lifestyle. In his discourse on John, Jesus draws our attention to the contrast between his temperament and ministry style when compared with that of his cousin.

> To what can I compare this generation? They are like children sitting in the marketplaces and calling out to others:
>
> "We played the pipe for you, and you did not dance; we sang a dirge, and you did not mourn."
>
> For John came neither eating nor drinking, and they say, "He has a demon." The Son of Man came eating and drinking, and they say, "Here is a glutton and a drunkard, a friend of tax collectors and sinners." But wisdom is proved right by her deeds. (Matthew 11:16–19)

These words of Jesus are the prelude to his lament over the unrepentant cities (Matthew 11:20–24). Despite their sharply contrasting lifestyles, this New Testament dynamic duo was unable to bring about the deep nationwide repentance both men sought. Furthermore, despite miraculous works, the population was largely unmoved, and therefore God's judgment would fall.[20]

Let's remember that the paramount goal for the prophetic Old Testament and New Testament dynamic duos is regime

[19] 2 Kings 6:1–7, 2 Kings 4:38–41, 2 Kings 4:42–44
[20] Matthew 11:23–24, Luke 19:41–44

change. And genuine regime change starts with repentance. Hearts must be changed. Repentance is entirely about a change in direction. The wayward and rebellious turn away from sin and toward God. A new King begins to reign in the repentant heart, and as a result a life is changed from the inside out. When this happens broadly in a society, a true Spirit-led awakening occurs.

Though Elijah was unable to bring about regime change, Elisha succeeded in doing just that, and he accomplished the transition in a remarkable way. He did it by commissioning an unnamed young man. Elisha entrusted the most significant nation-changing assignment of his career into the hands of a biblical nobody.

> And Elisha the prophet called one of the sons of the prophets, and said to him, "Get yourself ready, take this flask of oil in your hand, and go to Ramoth Gilead. Now when you arrive at that place, look there for Jehu the son of Jehoshaphat, the son of Nimshi, and go in and make him rise up from among his associates, and take him to an inner room. Then take the flask of oil, and pour it on his head, and say, 'Thus says the Lord: "I have anointed you king over Israel."' Then open the door and flee, and do not delay." (2 Kings 9:1–3, NKJV)

The young man did just as he was told. The result was the overthrow of a brutal dynasty that for three generations had led the nation into a cesspool of sin and the clutches of idolatry. The demonic yoke of Jezebel's oppression over Israel and Judah was broken, and the worship of the Lord was restored. This dramatic regime change was the culmination of the prophetic work of Elijah and Elisha.

Why did Elisha entrust this nation-changing assignment to this unnamed son of the prophets? Since Elisha received the revelation that regime change was at hand, why didn't he deliver the message himself? Why work through this nameless young man?

The answer lies in the character and ministry style of the prophet. Elisha was a man of humility and a team builder. He delegated responsibility rather than attempting to do everything himself. This team-building quality is displayed by his leadership role in the company of the prophets.[21] He continually worked with and alongside others, including his devious servant Gehazi.[22]

In his ministry style Elisha resembles Jesus, our Lord and Savior. Above all, Jesus was a humble team builder. Yes, like Elisha, he was a miracle-worker, but his most significant work (excluding redemption) was the education and equipping of his disciples. He too had his greedy Gehazi. His name was Judas Iscariot.[23] But Jesus risked all to train an army of followers who would overthrow the dark spiritual masters of this world and establish his kingdom. As Paul so eloquently states:

> For our struggle is not against flesh and blood, but against the rulers, against the authorities, against the powers of this dark world and against the spiritual forces of evil in the heavenly realms. (Ephesians 6:12)

Jesus deputized, empowered, and commissioned his followers to carry on his work, and he began doing so early in his ministry. He sent out the seventy (or in some translations, seventy-two) into the towns where he was about to go. They

---

[21] 2 Kings 6:1–7
[22] 2 Kings 5:19–27, 2 Kings 6:15–17
[23] John 12:4–6

returned rejoicing that the demons were subject to them. Their success brought Jesus great joy (see Luke 10:1–24).

Yes, Jesus has been using young, unsung, unnamed nobodies to accomplish his purpose from the very beginning.

11

ELIJAH'S "FLIGHT FROM WOMAN"

Then the man and his wife heard the sound
of the LORD God
as he was walking in the garden
in the cool of the day,
and they hid from the LORD God among
the trees of the garden.
But the LORD God called to the man,
"Where are you?"
(Genesis 3:8–9)

Before continuing to examine the typological link between Elisha and Jesus, a closer look at the low point in Elijah's ministry is warranted. We are all prone to temptation, and often we are blind to our own weaknesses. Thousands of reputable ministries have been tarnished or ruined after notable accomplishments.

It is remarkable how Elijah had great success in challenging the 450 prophets of Baal, calling down fire from heaven, and then having these false prophets put to death (1 Kings 18:20–

40). Finally, through prayer, he broke the three-year drought that had ravaged the land (Kings 18:41–46).

But after being cursed by Queen Jezebel, he ran away, becoming depressed and suicidal. How could just one woman have such a devastating impact on this hero of Israel? To what degree was she involved in the occult, and the manipulation of others through secret word curses?

> Now Ahab told Jezebel everything Elijah had done and how he had killed all the prophets with the sword. So Jezebel sent a messenger to Elijah to say, "May the gods deal with me, be it ever so severely, if by this time tomorrow I do not make your life like that of one of them." (1 Kings 19:1–2)

Jezebel believed she could destroy Elijah just like she destroyed many other men before him. But ultimately she did not finish well.[1]

In the Alcoholics Anonymous twelve-step program, the acronym H.A.L.T. is used to identify occasions when we are most vulnerable to temptation and even despair. Elijah suffered from all four temptations after his exhausting victory on Mount Carmel. His stunning success left him 1) Hungry 2) Angry 3) Lonely and 4) Tired.

What began as a flight from the woman Jezebel became a flight from God.

But God, in his compassion, ministered to Elijah's four needs, giving him food and drink, counsel, companionship, and sleep (1 Kings 19:3–9). Elijah's statement *"take my life"* (v. 4) is reminiscent of Jonah after his success in Nineveh, when he too did not want to live. In that loss of hope, God spoke to Elijah not

---

[1] 2 Kings 9:30–37

in the thunderstorm, earthquake, and pyrotechnics, but in that still small voice—the whisper of the Spirit (1 Kings 19:11–13).

The "flight from woman" and the LORD ended when Elijah started listening instead of just ranting at God.

> He replied, "I have been very zealous for the LORD God Almighty. The Israelites have rejected your covenant, torn down your altars, and put your prophets to death with the sword. I am the only one left, and now they are trying to kill me too." (1 Kings 19:14)

Elijah had to give up the lie that he was the only one left. Furthermore, in listening to God, Elijah had to admit that he was not ultimately in control.

One of Ed's heroes, E. Stanley Jones, listened to that still, small voice every day for one hour in the morning and one hour at night. He called it his listening post. Facing total burnout, Jones told God that he was done. God offered to take over if he would let go and let God order his life. He experienced Jesus' healing when he came to a deep self-surrender. Elijah on Mount Horeb similarly had to come to a self-surrender. Surrender is like death for spiritual superheroes like Elijah. It is the breaking point that is often needed so we can be fully yielded to God's will.

This "flight from woman" can be seen as representing a crisis in masculinity. The C.S. Lewis scholar Leanne Payne wrote a remarkable book by that very title, *Crisis in Masculinity*, which she dedicated to Dr. Karl Stern. He was a Montreal Jewish psychiatrist (and believer in Jesus) who wrote the 1965 book *Flight from Woman*.[2]

---

[2] "The *Flight from Woman* (1965), a philosophical treatise on modern society's polarization of the sexes and its de-feminization, would make him a common name in women's magazines." Deborah Ostrovsky, "The Freudian Became a Catholic," *Tablet*, August 24, 2014. https://www.tabletmag.com/sections/arts-letters/articles/karl-stern-freudian-catholic

Leanne Payne, mentored by the healing pioneer Agnes Sanford, had a remarkable ministry of bringing wholeness to broken people, particularly those struggling with identity issues. She saw that many men were running from the feminine, because they were in crisis with their own masculine identity. To Leanne, the image of Narcissus represented how many men curve in on themselves in self-worship.

Leanne was powerfully used to helping many men become whole through embracing their true identity as sons of the heavenly Father. Through healing prayer, Leanne Payne helped many recover the divine imagination and creativity that had been lost in their self-absorption. All of us need healing in areas where the image of God has been broken inside us. Powerful encounters with the Holy Spirit enable us to become more fully human. Such healing gives men the courage to responsibly embrace the unique challenges of marriage and family.

The crisis in masculinity has only deepened since the days of Payne and Stern. The identity confusion for young men is often paralyzing. The well-known Canadian psychologist Dr. Jordan Peterson often talks about how men are now the minority in universities, and how many of them are struggling to find direction and academic accomplishment. These difficulties often begin in the elementary grades, where all too often there are no male teachers, few positive male role models, and academic performance among boys has seen an alarming decline.

We are witnessing a well-documented male aversion to leadership. Both boys and men are refusing to assume the mantle of leadership.

In post-modernism, men are often defined as the problem. Our culture deconstructs people through guilt and shame, and then often leaves them in nihilistic despair. In contrast, the gospel gives hope to people.

While Jordan Peterson is not yet a Christ-follower, he has discovered how the Bible can help men be more authentic in living out their life's calling as responsible contributors. Healthy men fight for their families and marriages. They do not run from them. Healthy men sacrifice for their families. They don't sacrifice their wives and children on the altar of personal fulfillment and business success.

Elijah has much to teach men in our twenty-first-century context. Even after he ran from woman, he ultimately was found by God, and returned to face the challenges that God had set before him.

Hiding never works. It did not work for Adam and Eve, and it did not work for Elijah. Everyone loses when men hide from the responsibilities of life.

12

LIVING THE CRUCIFIED LIFE

I have been crucified with Christ;
it is no longer I who live, but Christ lives in me;
and the life which I now live in the flesh
I live by faith in the Son of God,
who loved me and gave Himself for me.
(Galatians 2:20, NKJV)

The Elisha Code is all about dying to self and living for Christ. Christ is the second Adam—the new man who fully bears the image of God. In Eden, the tempter succeeded in marring the image of God that was so beautifully evident in Adam and Eve before the fall. Sin robs and defiles. Jesus redeems and restores.

Two people who lived the crucified life were William Wilberforce and Corrie ten Boom. Both fought hatred and the dehumanizing forces of slavery and racism. Their most powerful weapon was relentless love. Today, those who embrace the Christ of the cross are called to do the same.

Abraham Lincoln once said that every school child should know about William Wilberforce.[1] For twenty long years from 1787 to 1807, Wilberforce persistently campaigned for the abolition of the slave trade. It was incredibly painful and often deeply discouraging work.

What kept him from giving up as he faced defeat after defeat? Wilberforce had previously lived a self-indulgent life as a very wealthy upper-class Englishman. What motivated him to stop wasting his life in drinking, gambling, and endless parties? He was a popular Member of Parliament who wowed crowds with his remarkable singing and wit. Prime Minister William Pitt said that Wilberforce had the greatest natural eloquence of all the men he had ever known.[2] What caused him to choose the unpopular path of putting principle above politics, and conscience over ambition?

With the death of Wilberforce's father at just age forty, William's comfortable world was radically shaken. At the age of eight, because of his mother's serious illness, he was shipped off to his Uncle William and Aunt Hannah in Wimbledon. Unbeknownst to his mother, he was mentored by Rev. John Newton, the former slave-ship captain and author of the song *Amazing Grace*. Some trace Wilberforce's hatred of slavery back to this earliest encounter.

When Wilberforce's wealthy grandfather got wind of his new spirituality, he threatened to disinherit him. So, Wilberforce's mother promptly rescued him and did her best to cure him through endless parties and upper-class

---

[1] Abraham Lincoln, "Lincoln on Abolition in England and the United States, 1858," *Gilder Lehman Institute of American History.* https://www.gilderlehrman.org/history-resources/spotlight-primary-source/lincoln-abolition-england-and-united-states-1858 (accessed April 13th 2023).

[2] Eric Metaxas, *Amazing Grace* (New York, NY: Harper Collins Publishers, 2007), 41.

distractions. For a while, the cure was effective. After his grandfather's death, Wilberforce inherited the family fortune, which funded his election as an eighteen-year-old member of parliament.

While spending the winter at the fashionable French and Italian Rivieras, he was suddenly called back to London in support of William Pitt's Parliamentary Reform Bill. While crossing the Swiss Alps, Wilberforce read *The Rise and Progress of Religion in the Soul* by Philip Doddridge. Both Doddridge and John Wesley were instrumental in reintroducing Richard Baxter's forgotten teachings about self-examination, solitude, devotions, and diligence.[3]

In discussing Doddridge's book with his former tutor Isaac Milner, Wilberforce's life was radically changed. He rediscovered his childhood faith at an adult level. Wilberforce, with Milner's assistance, began reading the Bible in the original Greek. He wanted to find out for himself what the Christian faith was truly about. He discovered that it was *not* a system of gloomy prohibitions. True faith is about peace and hope and joy. When Wilberforce fell in love with Jesus, he also fell in love with God's creation.

Rather than drop out of politics as he was tempted to do, Wilberforce turned his newfound faith into practical action. Prime Minister Pitt wrote him, saying: "Surely the principles as well as the practice of Christianity are simple, and lead not to meditation only but to action."[4]

Reconnecting with his old mentor, the converted slave-ship captain, John Newton, Wilberforce realized that God could use him to end the slave trade: "God Almighty has set before me

---

[3] William Hague, *William Wilberforce: The Life of the Great Anti-Slave Trade Campaigner* (London, UK: HarperCollins Publishers, 2007), 74.

[4] *The Private Papers of William Wilberforce*, (London: 1897), p. 13. Available at https://www.gutenberg.org/files/44912/44912-h/44912-h.htm.

two great objects: the suppression of the Slave Trade and the reformation of manners."[5]

Eighteenth-century England was rife with epidemic alcohol abuse, child prostitution, child labor, and animal exploitation. There were over 14,000 slaves in England alone, but hundreds of thousands more in the rich Caribbean English colonies, where slavery was out of sight and out of mind.[6] The future King of England George IV was famous for his immorality and gambling debts, keeping lockets of hair from all seven thousand women that he seduced.[7] The King and his royal brothers dismissed abolitionists like Wilberforce as fanatics and hypocrites.[8]

Because the English were the foremost slave-trading nation on earth, it was initially unthinkable for them to give it up. As one merchant accurately put it, the African slave trade was "the foundation of our commerce… the life of our navigation, and first cause of our national industry and riches."[9]

Eighty per cent of overseas British income came from the Caribbean slave plantations.[10] Wilberforce was naively asking England to commit commercial suicide. In Bristol, after the initial defeat of Wilberforce's bill, bells were rung, a bonfire was lit, and a half-day holiday was awarded to sailors and workers.[11] The passion for profit and slave-produced sugar had killed their conscience.

While fighting the slave trade, Wilberforce also invested in improving the life of England's poor, giving one quarter

---

[5] Available at https://www.bbc.co.uk/religion/religions/christianity/people/williamwilberforce_1.shtml, accessed August 25, 2023.

[6] Metaxas, *Amazing Grace*, 94.

[7] Metaxas, 72.

[8] Metaxas, 158.

[9] Hague, 119.

[10] Hague, 119.

[11] Hague, 225.

of his income—the equivalent of $300,000—away each year. He started cancer hospitals, eye clinics, and many faith-based schools for the poor.[12]

The slave trade was abolished in 1807; however, the slaves were not liberated until just before Wilberforce's death. On July 31, 1834, 800,000 Afro-Caribbeans were set free. While moving a motion for abolition, Wilberforce said, "Africa! Africa! Your sufferings have been the theme that has arrested and engages my heart—your sufferings no tongue can express; no language impart."[13]

In the 1940s, Corrie ten Boom also learned to act on her strong faith. The Nazis conquered the Netherlands in May, 1940, and during the German occupation, 100,000 Dutch Jews were sent to concentration camps. Corrie prayed, "Lord Jesus, I offer myself for your people. In any way. Any place. Any time."[14]

By disguising themselves as Nazi soldiers, her underground team saved one hundred Jewish babies from being killed in an orphanage. A well-known architect built them a secret two-and-a-half-foot-wide hiding place behind a new brick wall in Corrie's bedroom.[15] Even after arresting the ten Booms, the Gestapo were never able to find the Jews hidden in this "angel crib" hiding place.[16]

At the time of the arrest, Corrie's interrogator painfully slapped her in the face after every question. Corrie cried out: "Lord Jesus, protect me!"

He hissed at her, "If you mention that name again once more, I will kill you."

[12] Hague, 221.
[13] Metaxas, 151.
[14] Corrie ten Boom, *The Hiding Place* (New York, NY: Bantam Books, 1971), 114.
[15] Ten Boom, *The Hiding Place*, 120.
[16] Corrie ten Boom, *A Prisoner—And Yet* (London, UK: Christian Literature Crusade, 1954), 12.

But miraculously, he stopped beating her.[17]

Corrie and her sister Betsie hid over eight hundred Jewish people in their Haarlem watchmaker home, before being sent to Ravensbruck Concentration Camp in eastern Germany where 96,000 women died. "The sufferings of Jesus," said Corrie, "became very real to me at Ravensbruck."[18]

She lost four family members in the concentration camps, including her beloved older sister Betsie, who forgave and prayed for the guards even as they mercilessly beat her.

"Don't hate," Betsie pleaded to Corrie. Three days before Betsie died, she shared with Corrie the vision of opening healing homes in Holland and Germany, before going around the world sharing about Jesus' love and forgiveness. Two weeks later, Corrie was set free through a God-ordained clerical error.[19] One week after this, all the women her age at Ravensbruck were taken to be killed in the gas chamber.

Upon returning to Holland at the end of the war, Corrie opened a home to bring healing for people, including the ostracized Dutch collaborators. She was knighted by the Queen of the Netherlands for her work.

Corrie told God that she was willing to go where he wanted her to go, but hoped that he would never send her back to Germany. Finally, after sensing a blockage in her prayer life, she repented, saying, "Yes, Lord, I'll go to Germany too."[20]

God sent her back to Ravensbruck to lead Bible studies with former guards, now imprisoned there. Then, she rented and cleaned up a former concentration camp in Germany to bring temporary housing and healing to some of the nine

---

[17] Ten Boom, *A Prisoner—And Yet*, 13.

[18] Ten Boom, *A Prisoner—And Yet*, 87.

[19] Ten Boom, *The Hiding Place*, 241

[20] Corrie ten Boom, *Amazing Love* (London, UK: Christian Literature Crusade, London, 1954), 27.

million Germans who had been bombed or driven out of their homes.[21]

In 1946, a former Ravensbruck guard said to Corrie in Munich, "How grateful I am for your message, Fraulein. To think, as you said, that he washes my sins away!"

Corrie later wrote, "His hand was thrust out to shake mine… Even as angry, vengeful thoughts boiled through me, I saw the sin of them. Jesus Christ had died for this man. Was I going to ask for more? Lord Jesus, I prayed, forgive me and help me to forgive him… Again, I silently prayed 'Jesus, I cannot forgive him. Give me your forgiveness.' As I took his hand, my heart felt an overwhelming love for this stranger."[22]

Corrie became a penniless tramp for the Lord, travelling for three decades to sixty-two countries, and sleeping in over a thousand different beds.[23] Wherever she went globally, Corrie shared from her Ravensbruck experience that the light and love of Jesus Christ is deeper than the deepest darkness. She was the favorite travelling companion of the Bible-smuggler Brother Andrew as they both did missionary work behind the Iron Curtain, in Vietnam and in twelve other communist countries. In Vietnam, she was given the honorific title of "Double-Old Grandmother."

While in the Soviet Union, she intentionally preached the gospel in her hotel room, knowing that everything she said was being listened to and recorded by communist officials.

Through her deep friendship with Rev. Billy and Ruth Graham, Corrie's book *The Hiding Place* was turned into a movie that reached tens of millions.[24] Ruth Graham said, "I

---

[21] Ten Boom, *Amazing Love*, 36.

[22] Ten Boom, *The Hiding Place*, 238.

[23] Corrie ten Boom & Jamie Beckingham, *Tramp for the Lord* (BBS Publishing Company, New York, 1975, 1995), 185.

[24] James F. Collier, dir. *The Hiding Place*. World Wide Pictures, 1975. Distributed by BillyGraham.org.

didn't know anyone who had suffered so intensely for the Lord and for his people, as Corrie had, and come through with absolutely nothing but love in her heart for her captors—she forgave them."[25]

In 1967, Corrie was recognized by Israel as a Righteous Gentile, with the planting of a tree in her honor.[26] When people kept telling her how brave she was, Corrie transparently prayed, "What little courage I have… I was not brave. I was often like a timid, fluttering bird, looking for a hiding place… Lord, I am weak and cowardly and of little faith; do hold me close. Thou art the conqueror. May that assurance give me courage and loyalty."[27]

Because of her work blessing indigenous people, Corrie was adopted into the Hopi First Nation and given the name Beautiful Flower.[28] While staying at a Kansas farm, Corrie challenged her host, who had recently kicked his son out, telling him to never darken his doorstep again. She said to the farmer, "If you believe in Jesus Christ and belong to Him, your sins have been cast into the depths of the sea, and that's very deep. But then he expects also that you forgive the sins of your boy and cast them into the depths of the sea. Just imagine how you would feel if there should be another war, if your son had to go back into service and was killed in action. Don't you think you should forgive him right now?"

After riding together in silence, the farmer invited Corrie to go with him as he asked his son to forgive him. His son replied, "But Father, I should ask you for forgiveness."[29]

[25] Corrie ten Boom, "The Lives She Touched" video. Ruth Graham: "When I met Corrie, the thing that really impressed me was the twinkle in her eye. There was nothing but love and forgiveness."

[26] Ten Boom, *The Hiding Place*, 138.

[27] Ten Boom, *A Prisoner—and Yet*, 129.

[28] Corrie ten Boom, "The Lives She Touched" video.

[29] Ten Boom, *Amazing Love*, 10.

In her late sixties, Corrie was betrayed and hurt by some Christians she loved and trusted: "You would have thought that having been able to forgive the guards in Ravensbruck, forgiving Christian friends would be child's play. It wasn't. For weeks, I seethed inside. But at last, I asked God again to work His miracle in me… I was restored to the Father." She later burned the painful letters from her friends as a sign of letting go.[30]

Corrie ten Boom and William Wilberforce lived the crucified life. Unlike Adam and Eve, Wilberforce and ten Boom did not run from God. They found their hiding place in God (Psalm 32:7). In tumultuous times, they courageously fought against forms of racism that mar and debase the image of God that we all bear.

> So God created mankind in his own image; in the image of God he created them; male and female he created them. (Genesis 1:27)

---

[30] Ten Boom & Beckingham, *Tramp for the Lord*, 310.

13

THE GOD OF THE BROKEN

And He said,
"Your name shall no longer
be called Jacob, but Israel;
for you have struggled with God and
with men, and have prevailed."
(Genesis 32:28, NKJV)

The people whom God uses to change the world have first been radically changed by the Spirit of God. Often, these world-changers have experienced major setbacks. We might even say they have been broken by God, but they have come through those experiences transformed and empowered by the Spirit.

There is a pattern that emerges as we look back at the lives of the three revival leaders we have examined thus far. Each of them reached a breaking point.

A.B. Simpson was a successful minister who through much hard work built a large church, but he experienced burnout and a physical breakdown. From this low point, God healed him and raised him up to bring healing and salvation to thousands.

Similarly, Aimee Semple McPherson experienced a complete physical breakdown that left her hospitalized and at the point of death. She had returned from the mission field as a widow and a broken woman. She transitioned to a new life, but steadfastly resisted God's call. But God broke her resistance, miraculously restored her health, and catapulted her into a healing ministry that changed the trajectory of the church in America and the world.

Andrew Murray had what many would consider a successful ministry. But he too reached a breaking point. He lost his voice for two years. From this low point, God healed, transformed, and restored Murray to a far more effective and far-reaching ministry.

The common thread running through these life stories is that all three leaders encountered a breaking point. God broke them. Why would God do such a thing? Do *we* need to be broken to become effective ministers of the gospel of Christ?

There are several stories in the Bible that illustrate this need for God to break us.

The life story of the patriarch Jacob serves as the primary example. Jacob was a grasper. He grabbed for power. This is graphically illustrated by the way he came into this world. He arrived holding onto his twin brother's heel.[1] From the moment of birth, we see Jacob attempting to supplant Esau, his older brother, through cunning and deception.

Jacob succeeds first by trading a pot of lentil stew for Esau's birthright (Genesis 25:29–35), and later by conspiring with his mother to rob Esau of his father's blessing (Genesis 27:1–41). When Esau threatens to kill him, Jacob flees to the distant home of his uncle Laban.

Repeatedly, Jacob bargains with God, and God answers his prayers. Perhaps this is the most remarkable feature of Jacob's

---

[1] Genesis 25:21–26

life story. The LORD sticks with this deceiver and blesses him despite his devious ways. His life is a portrait of God's unmerited favor in the face of constant opposition.

Jacob meets his cunning, devious double in the person of Uncle Laban. First, Laban deceives Jacob by swapping Leah for her sister Rachel on his wedding night. There is more than a little divine justice at play in Laban's clever deception. Jacob, who cheated his blind father, is cheated blind in his own marriage bed. The irony in this outcome is striking. Jacob is required to work seven years for Leah and then seven more years for Rachel, his true love.[2]

Then, over the years, Laban changes Jacob's wages ten times. But despite Laban's constant readjustments, Jacob's flocks and herds grow and prosper. God's blessing, bestowed by Isaac, remains on Jacob.[3]

But eventually, God brings Jacob to a breaking point. It happens on Jacob's return to his homeland.

Jacob gets word that his brother Esau is coming to meet him with four hundred men. Why would Esau come with four hundred men unless he intended to carry out the death threat he uttered twenty years earlier? Suddenly, Jacob's life is on the line—and not only his life, but also the lives of his two wives, his daughter, and his twelve sons. His family and all the wealth he accumulated over years of hard labor are about to be wiped out. He finds himself in a truly desperate situation with no way out.

In exchange for his life, he offers to bargain away all his livestock, his wives, and his children. But will this desperate ploy satisfy the angry brother he has cheated? Jacob sends all he has ahead of him. To his servants he says:

---

[2] Genesis 29:14–30
[3] Genesis 31:38–42

When my brother Esau meets you and asks, "Who do you belong to, and where are you going, and who owns all these animals in front of you?" then you are to say, "They belong to your servant Jacob. They are a gift sent to my lord Esau, and he is coming behind us." (Genesis 32:17–18)

But Jacob stays back on the opposite side of the Jabok River. There, alone in the dark for the whole night, Jacob wrestles with a man. But in truth, he is wrestling with God.

Many Bible scholars view this man as a Christophany—a preincarnate appearance of Christ. Christ came down from heaven to break this obstinate cheater—break him and change him into a vessel he could use for his glory and his eternal purpose.

When the man saw that he could not overpower him, he touched the socket of Jacob's hip so that his hip was wrenched as he wrestled with the man. Then the man said, "Let me go, for it is daybreak."

But Jacob replied, "I will not let you go unless you bless me."

The man asked him, "What is your name?"

"Jacob," he answered.

Then the man said, "Your name will no longer be Jacob, but Israel, because you have struggled with God and with humans and have overcome."

Jacob said, "Please tell me your name."

But he replied, "Why do you ask my name?" Then he blessed him there.

So Jacob called the place Peniel, saying, "It is because I saw God face to face, and yet my life was spared." (Genesis 32:25–30)

There can be no doubt who the stronger man was at Peniel. With a simple touch, Jacob's hip was wrenched. With a simple touch, Christ would later heal the sick, raise the crippled, and restore sight to the blind. But here, Christ wrenched Jacob's hip and left him limping for the rest of his days.

Why this stark contrast? We can easily understand why Christ would heal a crippled beggar, but why would he break a man? Why break Jacob?

The simple answer is because Jacob needed to be broken. The wild horse serves no one. The wild stallion serves only himself. Only the broken horse is fit for the master's service. All of Jacob's service was self-serving, and that included his service to Laban. From Peniel onward, Jacob—broken Jacob—was serving the LORD.

David, the man after God's own heart, needed to be broken too. David was true to the LORD in the wilderness with jealous King Saul in hot pursuit, but after he assumed the throne of Israel, his fleshly desires led him astray. After his sin with Bathsheba, God needed to break him. The events that followed this sordid affair brought the humility so essential to effective service to God. Psalm 51 reflects the heart cry of a broken man.

This need for the servant of God to be broken by God appears in the New Testament as well. Peter needed to be broken by Jesus. Peter was a natural leader—sure of himself in all situations, ready to step out of a boat and even walk on water. That takes more than a little courage. But that confident self-assurance needed to be broken, and Jesus knew how to do it. It only took the crowing of a rooster to break Peter and reduce him to a blubbering, sobbing mess.

Jesus knows how to break the strongest men. But he also knows how to restore them.

Three times Jesus asked, *"Simon son of John, do you love me?"* (John 21:15–19).

Three times Peter affirmed his love for the Lord, and three times Jesus affirmed Peter's calling.

"Jesus said, 'Feed my lambs'" (v. 15).

"Jesus said, 'Take care of my sheep'" (v. 16).

"Jesus said, 'Feed my sheep'" (v. 17).

The broken Peter was now ready for service. He would fulfill the prophetic words Jesus had spoken over him before his fall and now in his restoration.

> Simon, Simon, Satan has asked to sift all of you as wheat. But I have prayed for you, Simon, that your faith may not fail. And when you have turned back, strengthen your brothers. (Luke 22:31–32)

The broken Peter had been humbled. Now Jesus ruled Peter. Now the Master was truly the Master and Lord of all.

Have you been broken by Jesus? Most Christians are eager to serve the Lord, but only in an advisory capacity. Peter was quick to give Jesus advice on how he should avoid the cross (see Matthew 16:21–27). But the Lord is not looking for our advice—he is looking for our obedience.

Jesus himself needed to be broken. His Heavenly Father broke him on the cross, from which he cried out, *"Eli, Eli, lema sabachthani?"* (*"My God, my God, why have you forsaken me?"*) (Matthew 27:46).

When Jesus broke, he broke the stranglehold of sin over humanity. His breaking was essential for the salvation of our souls.

As disciples of our Lord Jesus, we can expect to be broken as well. We need to become like our Master in every way.

Saul of Tarsus was zealous to serve the God of his fathers—
so zealous he persecuted the church. Jesus himself intervened
in Saul's life in order to break him. On the road to Damascus,
Saul was confronted by Jesus—arrested by Jesus—blinded and
broken by him.

Out of his brokenness, Saul, now renamed Paul, ministered
the gospel to the Gentile world of his day. Through his writing,
he continues to speak to millions today.

Have you been confronted by Jesus? Has he opposed you at
any point in your life? Have you been broken by him?

In the power of our own flesh, we can do many good and
noble things in the name of our Lord. Many fine churches have
been built through clever marketing and ingenuity. Human
effort and talent can carry us a long way.

In the eyes of many, A.B. Simpson had a successful ministry
before Christ broke him. Andrew Murray was powerfully used
by God before God broke him and set him aside for two years.
But both these men came out of their time of brokenness refined
and empowered by the Spirit of God. In their hearts, there had
been a regime change. The risen Christ was fully in charge now,
and the Spirit of God was directing them forward.

Are you and I ready to be broken and poured out at the
feet of Jesus?

Then Mary took a pound of very costly oil of spikenard,
anointed the feet of Jesus, and wiped His feet with her
hair. And the house was filled with the fragrance of the
oil. (John 12:3, NKJV)

14

THE CHURCH AND
THE THIRD TEMPTATION OF CHRIST

And He said to them,
"Render therefore to Caesar
the things that are Caesar's,
and to God the things that are God's."
(Matthew 22:21b, NKJV)

The church cannot move forward in the right direction unless there is a clear-eyed assessment of where we stand today.

Here then are a few questions to help us assess our current position:

- Are local churches growing, thriving, and multiplying in your city/community?
- Are individuals in your community repenting and coming to faith in Christ?
- Is the message of the gospel transforming society, or is the world transforming the church?

- Over the last twenty years, has the church become more politically engaged?

We have been keen observers of the church and the impact of the gospel on society for over fifty years. During that time there have been encouraging waves of numerical growth and spiritual renewal, but there have also been seasons of testing and decline. Broadly speaking, over the last decade, decline has been the dominant theme. Yes, there are exceptions to this downward trend, and they should be celebrated, but nevertheless, the trendline is not moving in our favor. Statistical surveys indicate a steady decline in church attendance and self-identification with the Christian faith.

Why is this so?

What has not declined is the church's level of political engagement. While the embers of spiritual revival have been dying, the fires of political engagement have been burning red hot. And political leaders of all stripes have been eager to fan the flames. After all, they know where the votes lie and how to spark political passions.

The sharp political divisions between the left and the right have been mirrored in the church. The theologically liberal have championed social justice issues, while theological conservatives have tried to hold the line against what they see as a sinful creeping socialist agenda.

To a degree, these divisions in the church have been present for generations. But in recent years the divisions have grown sharper as political discourse has become more polarized. Throw in some misinformation and a few conspiracy theories, and we have a toxic brew that social media spreads worldwide.

Where is the good news of the gospel in all of this? All too often, it has been abandoned or drowned out in both camps.

A worshipper may attend a Sunday service at a left-leaning church and hear a sermon on the merits of caring for the poor and marginalized, but the name of Jesus is never mentioned. Similarly, I have attended so called "prayer meetings" of evangelical pastors where not a single word of prayer is uttered, but the entire conversation is centered on right-wing political machinations and strategies.

Is the message of the gospel transforming our society and culture? No. The world is transforming the culture of the church. The glorious light of the gospel has been turned to darkness. Jesus' call to take up our cross and follow him is being ignored—ignored in the house of God while we pursue purely political objectives.

Christ's admonition rings true:

Salt is good; but if the salt has lost its flavor, how shall it be seasoned? It is neither fit for the land nor for the dunghill, but men throw it out. He who has ears to hear, let him hear! (Luke 14:34–35, NKJV)

The church has too often gone down a political rabbit hole, thinking it can somehow save this generation by political means. No such salvation exists—nor has it ever existed, and those who promise it are false saviors. Furthermore, Jesus prophesied such false political saviors would arise.

Then if anyone says to you, "Look, here is the Christ!" or "There!" do not believe it. For false christs and false prophets will rise and show great signs and wonders to deceive, if possible, even the elect. See, I have told you beforehand. (Matthew 24:23–25, NKJV)

Every generation has seen its share of false saviors, but after two thousand years, only one Savior remains standing. His name is Jesus. Let's cling to him and the message of the cross.

Often politicians use religion for personal gain—to curry favor and capture votes; therefore, leaders in the Christian community need to exercise caution. We believe Christ-followers should vote and be politically engaged—a life of service in the political realm can be a noble vocation ordained by God—but our first loyalty must be to Christ.

What blueprint did Jesus follow as he began his earthly ministry and set the foundation for the church? Was he engaged in the politics of his time? His politics was not the politics of this world. It was the politics of humility, forgiveness, and self-sacrifice.

The blueprint our Lord followed can be found in his response to the three temptations of Christ as recorded in the Gospels. The third temptation found in Matthew's Gospel specifically addresses the lure of political engagement.

> Again, the devil took Him up on an exceedingly high mountain, and showed Him all the kingdoms of the world and their glory. And he said to Him, "All these things I will give You if You will fall down and worship me."
>
> Then Jesus said to him, "Away with you, Satan! For it is written, 'You shall worship the LORD your God, and Him only you shall serve.'" (Matthew 4:8–10, NKJV)

There is something quite striking about both the devil's offer and Jesus' response. Satan offers the kingdoms of the world and their glory. Implied in this offer is the understanding that

THE ELISHA CODE & THE COMING REVIVAL

these kingdoms are currently his—under the devil's control. Jesus does not refute this. The nations are, in fact, within the devil's domain. This is in full agreement with Jesus' teaching on this matter, as he identified Satan as the *"prince of this world"* (John 12:30–33).

Similarly, Paul asserts that before their conversion the Ephesians *"walked according to the course of this world, according to the prince of the power of the air, the spirit who now works in the sons of disobedience…"* (Ephesians 2:2, NKJV).

Jesus refused Satan's offer of political power and reward if he would worship him. He refused to play on the devil's turf. He turned down the offer of earthly, political kingdoms so he could establish an eternal, spiritual kingdom—the kingdom of God.

Matthew ends his account of the three temptations of Christ with this statement: *"Then the devil left Him, and behold, angels came and ministered to Him"* (Matthew 4:11, NKJV). But Luke's account ends differently: *"When the devil had finished all this tempting, he left him until an opportune time"* (Luke 4:13).

Were there other occasions when Jesus was tempted to become politically engaged and establish an earthly kingdom? There may have been numerous occasions, but three are readily identifiable.

John identifies one such occasion immediately after the feeding of the five thousand.

> Then those men, when they had seen the sign that Jesus did, said, "This is truly the Prophet who is to come into the world."
>
> Therefore when Jesus perceived that they were about to come and take Him by force to make Him king, He departed again to the mountain by Himself alone. (John 6:14–15, NKJV)

What a grand opportunity this was! Jesus could have become king. Furthermore, it would not have had the appearance of something he had sought. He could simply have bowed to the will of the people, and they would have proclaimed him king.

You can almost hear the devil's whisper, "These are good people. They recognized you as the Prophet. Now, they want to make you king. Surely, this must be the will of God."

But what did Jesus do? Did he accept the devil's latest offer? No. He walked away. Instead of making a deal with the world and the devil, Jesus went to pray in a lonely place where he met with his Father. He walked away from an earthly political kingdom and all its trappings. Wealth. Fame. Adoration.

Why walk away?

For a second time Jesus walked away from a temporal, material kingdom because he was establishing an eternal, spiritual kingdom—a kingdom that exists on a much higher plane than the kingdoms of this world.

And after a time of communion with his Father, what did Christ do?

He walked on water.

The juxtaposition of these events was not due to random chance. Jesus walked out on the Sea of Galilee to visibly demonstrate the spiritual nature of his eternal kingdom. The disciple's initial reaction illustrates this perfectly.

> Shortly before dawn Jesus went out to them, walking on the lake. When the disciples saw him walking on the lake, they were terrified. "It's a ghost," they said, and cried out in fear. (Matthew 14:25–26)

Jesus was entirely at home in the spirit world, but we are not. The disciples reacted just as we would. The truth we must lay hold of is the spiritual nature of Christ and his kingdom. By faith Peter briefly grasped that truth as he stepped out of the boat, and he too walked on water.

Oh, for the faith to do likewise in this day and hour! Are we ready to do as Peter did—to step into the supernatural and walk in the Spirit?

The second occasion when Jesus was tempted to take a political position is well known. It occurred within the temple courts during the last week of his earthly ministry.

> Then the Pharisees went and plotted how they might entangle Him in His talk. And they sent to Him their disciples with the Herodians, saying, "Teacher, we know that You are true, and teach the way of God in truth; nor do You care about anyone, for You do not regard the person of men. Tell us, therefore, what do You think? Is it lawful to pay taxes to Caesar, or not?"
>
> But Jesus perceived their wickedness, and said, "Why do you test Me, you hypocrites? Show Me the tax money."
>
> So they brought Him a denarius.
>
> And He said to them, "Whose image and inscription is this?"
>
> They said to Him, "Caesar's."
>
> And He said to them, "Render therefore to Caesar the things that are Caesar's, and to God the things that are God's." When they had heard these words, they marveled, and left Him and went their way. (Matthew 22:15–22, NKJV)

The Pharisees were certain they could trap Jesus on the horns of this dilemma. Note that to execute their devious scheme, the Pharisees teamed with a political party, the Herodians. In this situation, politics and religion conspired together, and undoubtedly Satan was the one who chaired this meeting.

The exact wording of this question is significant. The question could have been, "Is it lawful to pay taxes to Rome, or not?" Or perhaps, "Is it lawful to pay taxes to the Empire, or not?" Why this direct reference to Caesar?

The question as asked goes to the very heart of the Jewish faith, and the Christian faith as well. Caesar was a deity in the Roman pantheon of gods. By paying taxes to Caesar, were Jewish believers violating the first commandment of the law of Moses? Were they participating in the worship of a foreign god? To the devout Jew, the image of Caesar on a Roman coin was a graven image signifying idolatry. For this reason, Roman coinage, the denarius, was not accepted in the temple treasury. It had to be converted to Tyrian shekels—hence the need for moneychangers in or near the temple courts.

If Jesus said it was wrong to pay taxes to Caesar, he could be accused of supporting the zealots who advocated rebellion against Rome. If he approved of tax payment, he left himself vulnerable to the charge of violating the first commandment and the worship of a foreign god.

How does Jesus solve the dilemma? His answer can be described as a brilliant sidestep. It allows for tax payment and allegiance to both God and Caesar. But...

But we need to qualify this statement. Supremacy and first allegiance belong to the Lord. To put our allegiance to the nation state on an equal footing with our allegiance to God runs contrary to the counsel of Christ and the Scriptures. Note well our Savior's words:

> No one can serve two masters; for either he will hate
> the one and love the other, or else he will be loyal to the

one and despise the other. You cannot serve God and mammon. (Matthew 6:24, NKJV)

Though the reference above contrasts service to God and service to mammon (money/material possessions), the implications of having two masters are clear. One master must take precedence. Is it God or money? Is it God or the state? Is it God or the political leader or party?

Far too many believers have divided loyalties, when Christ demands our all. A weak-kneed gospel requires little from us, but in truth, Jesus demands everything.

Now great multitudes went with Him. And He turned and said to them, "If anyone comes to Me and does not hate his father and mother, wife and children, brothers and sisters, yes, and his own life also, he cannot be My disciple. And whoever does not bear his cross and come after Me cannot be My disciple." (Luke 14:25–27, NKJV)

God and Caesar are not on an equal footing. And dual loyalty on an equal basis is not what Christ is advocating for in his discussion with the Pharisees and the Herodians. He is conceding that submission to civil authorities is required.

In his teaching on the command to honor father and mother, Martin Luther expands the scope of those to whom honor and obedience are due. He includes "masters" and goes on to define them as follows: "Masters are all those who by God's ordinance are placed over us in the home, in the state, at the school and at the place where we work."[1]

---

[1] *Luther's Small Catechism: A Handbook of Christian Doctrine* (St. Louis, MO: Concordia Publishing House), 64.

Luther saw in the Ten Commandments a hierarchy of submission and obedience that begins with God and extends through the family, the workplace, and the state.

Jesus' answer makes it clear that he is not leading a political rebellion—a rebellion against Rome. He is not taking the devil's bait. Since the foundation of the world, the devil has been the author and master of rebellion. For this reason, Christians must exercise due diligence and hear from God before throwing in their lot with those who advocate the overthrow of established authorities. If those authorities are established by God, we may find ourselves working against the God we serve.

There are multiple examples in the Scriptures where God called for submission to authority, even heathen authority, rather than rebellion. The classic example is the Jewish people's submission to foreign rule during their seventy years of captivity in Babylon. After urging the captives to build homes and raise families, the prophet Jeremiah gave the exiles these instructions:

> Also, seek the peace and prosperity of the city to which I have carried you into exile. Pray to the LORD for it, because if it prospers, you too will prosper. (Jeremiah 29:7)

While serving in a position of submission to ungodly autocrats, leaders such as Daniel and Nehemiah laid the groundwork for the return to the holy land, and the restoration of the Jewish state and temple worship. This is not the outcome one would expect from yielding to the authority of a pagan government. However, we need to recognize there is a much higher authority who oversees the affairs of all humanity. Surely, this proverb holds true: *"In the LORD's hand the king's heart is a stream of water that he channels toward all who please him"* (Proverbs 21:1).

Jesus displayed impeccable wisdom in his response to the politically charged question of taxation. But his wise response did not prevent his arrest, trial, and crucifixion. And what were the charges brought against him?

> Then the whole assembly rose and led him off to Pilate. And they began to accuse him, saying, "We have found this man subverting our nation. He opposes payment of taxes to Caesar and claims to be Messiah, a king." (Luke 23:1–2)

The charges before Pontius Pilate were entirely political. Let's remember that another name for Satan is "the accuser," and he is only too eager to use human vessels to convey his accusations. Furthermore, why not use an outright lie, since he is the father of lies?[2]

Following the feeding of the five thousand, Jesus rejected the role of an earthly king, and later, he explicitly endorsed the payment of taxes to Caesar, yet the master of lies and distortion accused him of both these political infractions. The devil never plays fair. In Christ's trial before Pilate, Satan manipulated the high priest, the crowd, and all the players to achieve his goal—the death of Jesus.[3]

Throughout his ministry, Jesus steadfastly resisted political entanglement, but in the end, the accusation of political ambition was precisely what Satan used to bring about Christ's crucifixion.

Finally, let's examine the third occasion when Jesus was tempted to become politically engaged and establish an earthly

---

[2] John 8:44

[3] For a thorough play-by-play account of the trial and crucifixion of Christ, and the political machinations of Herod Antipas, Joseph Caiaphas, and Pontius Pilate, read *The Soldier Who Killed a King* by David Kitz (Kregel Publications, 2017).

kingdom. The location was Gethsemane. After agonizing several hours in prayer, Jesus rose to meet his betrayer. John tells us that Peter came to Christ's defense, and in the ensuing fracas Peter cut off the ear of the servant of the high priest.

> "Put your sword back in its place," Jesus said to him, "for all who draw the sword will die by the sword. Do you think I cannot call on my Father, and he will at once put at my disposal more than twelve legions of angels? But how then would the Scriptures be fulfilled that say it must happen in this way?"
>
> In that hour Jesus said to the crowd, "Am I leading a rebellion, that you have come out with swords and clubs to capture me? Every day I sat in the temple courts teaching, and you did not arrest me. But this has all taken place that the writings of the prophets might be fulfilled." Then all the disciples deserted him and fled. (Matthew 26:52–56)

It is clear from the passage above that Jesus was continually tempted to reverse his arrest, trial, and crucifixion. Twelve legions of angels were standing ready to do just that. At any moment, by a dramatic show of force, he could have overpowered any adversary. Why endure the coming humiliation, torture, and death?

Jesus provides the answer to this question in this statement, *"But this has all taken place that the writings of the prophets might be fulfilled."* Jesus was moving according to a plan established in eternity, revealed by the prophets, and prepared well in advance. Nothing was happening by chance. During this Passover celebration, the sacrificial Lamb of God would lay down his life. His redeeming blood would stain a cross to wash away the stains of our corrosive sin.

Jesus had prepared his heart in prayer. He had heard his Father's voice. He had to drink this bitter cup of suffering, and nothing would deter him. Not the comforts of the flesh. Not the temptations of the world. Not the demons of hell.

The temptation for Jesus to call on legions of angels for deliverance combines aspects of the three wilderness temptations described in Matthew chapter four. It brings comfort to the body rather than excruciating torture—the first temptation. It appeals to the desire for fame, self-promotion, and the spectacular—the second temptation. And finally, it holds the promise of a political victory over an oppressive enemy. Why not call on the angels? Why not establish Christ's immediate supremacy over his earthly foes? The angels had ministered to him after his forty-day fast and temptation in the wilderness. Why not call on them now?

The answer lies in the nature of the King and the nature of his kingdom. Jesus is God by nature and coequal within the Trinity. Yes, he was and is fully human, but he is simultaneously fully eternal and divine. This King has no beginning and no end, and his power and authority have no limits. Holiness is the foundation of his throne.

But this same King—this same Jesus—came to the cross in full submission to his Father. He took the lowest position. Jesus became the least in the kingdom of God, being willing to suffer humiliation and a criminal's death on the cross.[4]

Was Jesus leading a rebellion against the political authorities of his day? The answer is a resounding "No!"

But in his human flesh, he was leading a rebellion to unseat the most powerful earthly ruler of all time, *the prince of the power of the air.* How did Christ defeat him?

Jesus defeated Satan by becoming the exact opposite of his foe. The chief characteristics of Satan are pride and rebellion. To

[4] Matthew 11:11

defeat the master of pride and rebellion, Jesus took on the form of a servant.[5] He humbled himself to the lowest place—the place of the cross—and from that position he crushed the head of the ancient serpent.

At his Last Supper, Jesus demonstrated his servanthood by washing his disciples' feet.[6] He clearly taught the principle of humble submission.

> Now there was also a dispute among them, as to which of them should be considered the greatest. And He said to them, "The kings of the Gentiles exercise lordship over them, and those who exercise authority over them are called 'benefactors.' But not so among you; on the contrary, he who is greatest among you, let him be as the younger, and he who governs as he who serves. For who is greater, he who sits at the table, or he who serves? Is it not he who sits at the table? Yet I am among you as the One who serves.
>
> "But you are those who have continued with Me in My trials. And I bestow upon you a kingdom, just as My Father bestowed one upon Me, that you may eat and drink at My table in My kingdom, and sit on thrones judging the twelve tribes of Israel." (Luke 22:24–30, NKJV)

How will we defeat and disarm Satan and lay waste to his kingdom? It will not happen through mere political engagement. That is not the route Jesus took. That political rabbit hole leads to the devil's lair. We are intruding on Satan's turf when we head down that hole, and he knows how to fight and win down there. He has been doing it for thousands of years.

---

[5] Philippians 2:5–11
[6] John 13:1–17

We win by using the same tactics as Jesus. It is the surrendered life that wins battles in the spiritual realm. It is the life surrendered to the will of the Father that prepares the way for salvation and world-transforming revival.

15

PROPHETIC VOICES FOR OUR TIME

Now in the church at Antioch
there were prophets and teachers:
Barnabas, Simeon called Niger,
Lucius of Cyrene, Manaen
(who had been brought up with Herod
the tetrarch) and Saul.
(Acts 13:1)

Are there modern-day prophets, or did that all cease when the Bible was completed? Prophecy will cease one day when Jesus, the perfect one, returns to take us home (1 Corinthians 13:10). But clearly Paul saw a vital role for prophets in the New Testament church. He and Barnabas were sent out on their first missionary journey by the prophets and teachers in Antioch.[1] Paul saw prophets as Christ-appointed and Christ-ordained.

> So Christ himself gave the apostles, the prophets, the evangelists, the pastors and teachers, to equip his people for works of service, so that the body of Christ

---

[1] Acts 13:1–3

> may be built up until we all reach unity in the faith
> and in the knowledge of the Son of God and become
> mature, attaining to the whole measure of the fullness
> of Christ. (Ephesians 4:11–13)

In our time, we have seen evidence of prophets among us. Sometimes, those prophets emerge from an unlikely place—from the wilderness, even the Siberian wilderness. A key example is Alexander Solzhenitsyn, who challenged both eastern and western regimes and politicians. As Solzhenitsyn became world-renowned, he was being "played" by the politicians and other writers, just like Jesus was tempted in the wilderness. Everyone wanted to claim him as their own, without really hearing his prophetic challenge.

Solzhenitsyn was sent to a Siberian prison for ten years, because he dared to question Joseph Stalin in a private letter to a friend. While in prison, he wrote the first book to be published about the communist Siberian prisons: *One Day in the Life of Ivan Denisovich*. Not allowed to write due to extreme censorship, he had to store the book in his brain, and only recorded it on paper much later.

The Soviet leader Nikolai Khrushchev, who resented Stalin's abuses, publicly criticized Stalin, and then welcomed Solzhenitsyn's book since it supported his new stance. His official authorization of this book was mind-boggling for the Soviets. This was the initial crack in the formidable Iron Curtain.

After Khrushchev was deposed, however, the repression came back, and Solzhenitsyn was shut down again. He had to write in secret, hiding his writings in bottles, buried in the ground. He was in real trouble with the Soviets over the publication of his book *Cancer Ward*, after he survived terminal cancer. In Russia, everything was supposed to be wonderful. How dare he criticize the perfect socialist society? The KGB poisoned him in 1971, but he miraculously survived.

When he wrote two copies of *The Gulag Archipelago*, the KGB stole one of the copies, which had been hidden by a friend. After they tortured her and she gave it up, she hung herself. With the other copy, he could wait no longer, so in 1973, he sent it to be published in the West.

Often the finest gold is refined in the furnace of affliction, and the Siberian gulag was certainly a furnace of affliction.[2]

Solzhenitsyn was treated as a traitor in Russia. But West Germany accepted him, after he was thrown out of the Soviet Union.

When Solzhenitsyn moved to Vermont, USA, to write in seclusion, the media showered him with unrelenting adulation. The peak of this attention was his speech at a 1978 commencement event to 20,000 people outside in the rain at Harvard University. It was the largest gathering at Harvard in known history.

The crowd expected that he would give a pleasant talk criticizing Russia and complimenting the West over its stand for freedom. Instead, he spoke about Harvard's motto Veritas, affirming objective, knowable truth. In his talk, he prophetically critiqued Western culture and the USA for its softness and lack of courage. He shocked them by saying that he could not commend the West to Russia because of its self-indulgence.

He said that because the Russian Christians suffered so deeply under communism, they developed more spiritually. In contrast, the West had worshipped material success, but often ignored its spiritual development. From that point on, the media treated Solzhenitsyn as a non-person, barely mentioning

---

[2] Isaiah 48:9–11

him. What was his offence? He failed to endorse the Cold War political narrative; instead he addressed the spiritual poverty in America.

Solzhenitsyn challenged us prophetically to embrace the cross, rather than western material success. Have we heeded his call? No—individually and as a society we have continued to plunge headlong into a pursuit of happiness through material wealth. Surely the next raise, the next trinket, the next high-tech gadget will bring us happiness.

Often, the church has simply mimicked our society's worldly pursuit of prosperity. Of course, we have sanctified the language of greed by calling it God's blessing. But true spiritual wealth is not measured by a bank account or a nation's GDP. Spiritual wealth is measured on the scales of eternity by our adherence to God's truth and God's will.

The words of Jesus to the church of Laodicea ring true for us today:

> You say, "I am rich; I have acquired wealth and do not need a thing." But you do not realize that you are wretched, pitiful, poor, blind and naked. I counsel you to buy from me gold refined in the fire, so you can become rich; and white clothes to wear, so you can cover your shameful nakedness; and salve to put on your eyes, so you can see.
>
> Those whom I love I rebuke and discipline. So be earnest and repent. (Revelation 3:17–19)

Frequently throughout history the true prophets have been rejected. Consider the life and ministry of Jeremiah, for example.[3] The true prophet does not tell us what we want to hear; rather, he tells us what we need to hear.

---

[3] Jeremiah 1:4–6

Elijah and Elisha called the people of Israel to repent. At the start of the New Testament era, John the Baptist and Jesus did the same.

Are we ready and willing to heed their call to repent? Will we heed the prophets of our time who challenge us to humble ourselves and return to the Lord?

16

PREPARING A LANDING STRIP
FOR THE HOLY SPIRIT

And this was his message:
"After me comes the one more powerful than I,
the straps of whose sandals I am not worthy
to stoop down and untie.
I baptize you with water, but he will
baptize you with the Holy Spirit."
(Mark 1:7–8)

The title of this chapter is a present-day metaphor that aptly describes the ministry mandate of John the Baptist as found in the Gospels. John was preparing a landing strip for the spiritual revival that Jesus launched.

> …as it is written in Isaiah the prophet: "I will send my messenger ahead of you, who will prepare your way"—"a voice of one calling in the wilderness, 'Prepare the way for the Lord, make straight paths for him.'" (Mark 1:2–3)

John was the way-maker for Jesus. With his message of repentance followed by baptism, John prepared the ground for the great revival that occurred under the ministry of Jesus. John was Act One in this great drama of the ages. Jesus was Act Two. And via the Holy Spirit, the apostles are featured in Act Three, and of course, we read of their accomplishments in the book of Acts. But the book of Acts has no end. The work of the Holy Spirit continues to this present day.

John the Baptist and Jesus were revivalists—the greatest revivalists of all time. This dynamic New Testament duo set in motion a whole series of revivals that stretch down through the ages and continue to this day.

Remarkably, John the Baptist glimpsed all this. Operating in the prophetic realm, he predicted that Jesus would baptize his followers with the Holy Spirit. That prediction was fulfilled on the day of Pentecost, when the Holy Spirit was poured out on those who were gathered in the upper room (Acts 2:1–4).

Oh, how we need an upper room experience—a baptism in the Holy Spirit experience!

It has been said that the Holy Spirit is like a jet plane. Jet planes cannot land just anywhere. They need a properly prepared runway.

Did any preparation precede the coming of the Holy Spirit on the day of Pentecost? Yes, there was a good deal of preparation. Jesus gave his disciples this specific command:

Do not leave Jerusalem, but wait for the gift my Father promised, which you have heard me speak about. For John baptized with water, but in a few days you will be baptized with the Holy Spirit. (Acts 1:4b–5)

The disciples obeyed Jesus' command. They spent ten days gathered in prayer, waiting for the coming of the Holy Spirit.

Their hearts were yearning for what the Master promised. This was preparation time.

Are you and I eagerly anticipating the coming of the Holy Spirit into our lives with power? Are we hungry for God? Are we expecting the mighty rush of the Holy Spirit to swoop down into our lives? Have we prepared the runway with prayer? Are we pregnant with expectant faith?

The Holy Spirit comes to prepared hearts, and he is actively engaged even now in the business of preparing hearts. Is the Spirit preparing the runway of your heart for the moment of touchdown?

Times of revival often bring an unexpected wave of Christ-centered fervency among young people who have been lost in the world system. This has been true throughout the ages. In the notable revivals of the last century, young people were at the forefront.

In desperate times, God often shows up, surprising everyone.

Many young people today struggle with hopelessness. Even free drugs from government agencies are not solving the plague of tragic opioid deaths. There is an emptiness in the lives of many youths that only God can fill. Times of revival involve the prophesied turning of the hearts of the young back to their fathers and to the living God. This is really a return to one of the core truths of the Elisha Code.

> See, I will send the prophet Elijah to you before that great and dreadful day of the Lord comes. He will turn the hearts of the parents to their children, and the hearts of the children to their parents; or else I will come and strike the land with total destruction. (Malachi 4:5–6)

We, David Kitz and Ed Hird, are an example of a dynamic duo writing about biblical dynamic duos. We have many things in common, such as our experience in charismatic renewal and the Jesus movement, and our similar Lutheran and Anglican heritage. We were teenagers and college students when God poured his Spirit out upon both of us again and again.

Both of us experienced the joy of being fully immersed, something that happened frequently during the Jesus movement at seaside beaches, lakesides, and church baptistries. Full immersion baptism was one of the defining features of the Jesus movement. Why was that the case?

It really was a full-blown return to first-century Christianity. The key verse we heard quoted repeatedly during that time was drawn from Peter's sermon on the day of Pentecost.

Then Peter said to them, "Repent, and let every one of you be baptized in the name of Jesus Christ for the remission of sins; and you shall receive the gift of the Holy Spirit." (Acts 2:38, NKJV)

We saw ourselves as living and re-enacting the New Testament. The miracle of rebirth was our new reality.

The Jesus movement was preceded by the hippie movement, which brought 100,000 youth to Haight-Ashbury in San Francisco for the 1967 Summer of Love. But by the end of 1969, many had died from drug overdoses. Then in December 1969, a young man was stabbed to death at a free rock concert in Altamont, California. Out of the ashes of the failed hippie dream of free love and peace, the Jesus movement unexpectedly emerged.

Looking back, we can see there are some striking similarities between our current situation and the social and political climate of the late 1960s and early 1970s. We live in a time of sharp division and social and political upheaval. Everywhere, long-established norms are being questioned and jettisoned. Many would say we have lost our moorings and are drifting in a dangerous current with no sense of direction. The same was true in the late 1960s and early 1970s. With the Vietnam War raging and sharp divisions between the generations, many found themselves at a social and emotional breaking point.

Jesus stepped into the mess of that time, and we are confident he will step into the upheaval and mess of our time as well.

With the recent Asbury revival[1] and the release of *The Jesus Revolution* movie, we are reminded of the vitality of the 1970s Jesus movement. An estimated three million young people entered the kingdom during this remarkable season of refreshing. It had a profound effect on the culture of that time. Revival is often a small thing when it breaks out, but it spreads like a prairie fire.

This was a fresh Spirit-prompted awakening with unique characteristics. It was a movement that spread from the bottom up. It sprang up spontaneously with no central theme or figure except the Lord Jesus. In the beginning, it had no defined leadership, though eventually various leaders emerged. Though it began on the West Coast and maintained a West Coast vibe, it soon hitchhiked across the continent and marshalled young Jesus followers in diverse communities and every major city.

Like previous awakenings, the Jesus movement changed the music and the prevailing culture of that time.

A word of caution is warranted. The "Jesus people" grew and filled many churches to overflowing in the early 1970s. But at the same time, many churches were largely unaffected. Churches in decline often continued to decline. The tide of revival did not lift all boats.

---

[1] "LIVE from Asbury University's Spiritual Revival," *CBN News*. https://www.youtube.com/watch?v=4IZL9d-g_fc&t=154s

Why was that the case?

Some churches welcomed these radical young Jesus followers, while others scoffed at their newfound faith, seeing it as only a passing fad. For some who were swept up in the moment, that criticism was valid. The devil is only too eager to snatch away the word that falls along life's path so it cannot take root. But for those who were received into fellowship and grew in their love for the Lord and the Word of God, the impact was transformative and lifelong.

If revival breaks out among young people today, will our churches be ready and welcoming, or will our response be negativity and criticism? We need to position ourselves to receive what the Holy Spirit brings our way. It may look different than what we expect.

Sometimes a revival, like the Jesus movement, comes completely out of the blue. Similarly, no one planned or expected the latest Asbury outpouring among college students.

So many tens of thousands poured into this six-thousand-person college town in Wilmore, Kentucky, that police had to post highway signs saying, "Revival Over Capacity."

Asbury College has had many youth revivals over the years: 1905, 1908, 1921, 1950, 1958, 1970, 1992, 2006, and now 2023. One of our heroes, Dr. E. Stanley Jones, experienced the Asbury revival of joy and holy laughter in 1905, before being sent to India as a missionary for the next fifty years. He commented:

> …suddenly we were all swept off our feet by a visitation of the Holy Spirit. We were all filled, flooded by the Spirit. Everything that happened to the disciples on the original Pentecost happened to us.[2]

---

[2] E. Stanley Jones, *A Song of Ascent* (Nashville, TN: Abingdon Press, 1979), 68.

Jones spoke about being calmly intoxicated with God's love:

> For three or four days, it could be said of us as was said of those at the original Pentecost. "They are drunk." I was drunk with God... For three days, there were no college classes... I saw into the heart of reality, and the heart of reality was joy, joy, joy. And the heart of reality was love, love, love.[3]

Asbury, said Jones, had both the "warmed heart" and the "world parish" missionary passion.[4] Acts 1:8 reminds us that outpouring precedes outgoing. God is similarly raising up many young people in the current outpouring who will go to the ends of the earth with the good news.

Once you have a taste of revival, it leaves you longing for more. God willing, Jesus movement veterans like us may have the privilege of living through several coming revivals. We pray that we will be humble enough to have eyes to see, and not reject, coming youth revivals just because they may look different than what we remember.

Come Holy Spirit in revival fire. Touch down on the young generation. Land the jetliner of your presence with the sound of a mighty rushing wind.

---

[3] Jones, *A Song of Ascent*, 69.

[4] Jones, 67.

17

FINISHING WELL AND GROWING IN FRUITFULNESS

God will bless you,
if you don't give up when your faith
is being tested.
He will reward you with a glorious life,
just as he rewards everyone who loves him.
(James 1:12, CEV)

C.S. Lewis memorably commented, "You are never too old to set another goal or to dream a new dream."[1]

The dynamic duo of Elijah and Elisha were always being stretched by God to set another goal and dream another dream. God wanted both to finish well, not peter out.[2] You will remember how Elijah was ready to give up on being faithful. He had lost sight of his ongoing calling from God prior to calling his successor Elisha.

---

[1] "C. S. Lewis Quote on How You Are Never Too Old To Give Direction To Your Life," *MoveMe Quotes* (https://movemequotes.com/c-s-lewis-quote/, accessed March 15, 2023).

[2] E. Stanley Jones, *Mastery* (Nashville, TN: Abingdon Press, 1955), 324.

What if, instead of giving up, we gave over? Surrender to the will of God is always the way forward. If there is breath in our lungs, God still has something for his servants to do. We are never to stop serving others until the Lord takes us home. Never stop learning, reading, and listening. Do you still have fire in your bones to make a difference? Would you like to get your fire, your zest for living, back?

Both Ed Hird and David Kitz have presided over many funerals over the past decades of ordained ministry. When we hear the funeral eulogies from family members, it often makes us wish that we had known the deceased better. Many people wait until the loved one is dead to say how much they loved them. We often wonder: "Why wait?" Part of finishing well is having a faithful team cheer as you aim for the finish line.

One of Ed's favorite mentors, Dr. E. Stanley Jones, entered his fifties by deciding that it would be the most fruitful decade of his life thus far, and it was. When he turned sixty, seventy, and then eighty, he continued to declare that the next decade was once again going to exceed the previous one, and it did. While he was officially "retired" by the Methodist Board of Missions in 1954, he went on to have a remarkably fruitful phase of ministry for almost two more decades. In 1963, for instance, he preached 736 times. Jones deeply lived out Psalm 92:14: *"They still bring forth fruit in old age, they are ever full of sap and green"* (RSV).

Stanley Jones reminds people in his twenty-eight books that there is no such thing as retirement from a biblical perspective. Retreading, recycling, repositioning, yes. But we can never retire from being fruitful in life and making a lasting difference. "Never retire," said Jones, "change your work. The human personality is made for creation; and when it ceases to create, it creaks, and cracks, and crashes."[3]

[3] Ibid.

Creativity is at the heart of staying fully alive. Without growing in creativity, we shrink and become less human—less Christlike.

When Ed left St. Simon's North Vancouver after serving for thirty-one years, he intentionally did not have a retirement party, but rather a "new chapter of ministry" party. In our current culture, we often do not do transitions well.

What new chapter are you currently writing in the book of your life? Are you stuck in any way? Is it time to turn the page? As his departure drew near Paul wrote, *"I have fought the good fight, I have finished the race, I have kept the faith"* (2 Timothy 4:7). Paul persevered in triumphant faith till the end.

Many pastors do not finish well when they get older. They may become grumpy, critical, and negative. With aging, we have our aches and pains, and we must work harder at being positive. David recently preached a message on "The glass half-full or glass half-empty." When you are older, it is easier to be negative, to be a no-centered person. E. Stanley Jones said that we are not as old as our arteries, but rather our attitudes.[4] Are you growing in becoming a more positive, thankful person?

Dr. Martin Gumpert, in his book *You are Younger than You Think*, says that "idleness is the greatest enemy of the aged and presents them with their ticket to death."[5]

When the retirement age of sixty-five was introduced by the United States in the 1930s, the average man only lived eighteen months after retirement. It was too much of a shock to their systems to cease productive activity.

The Alcoholics Anonymous *Big Book* comments that many people never become alcoholic until they retire. They say to themselves, "I've worked hard all my life. Now I will do what

---

[4] Ibid., 327.

[5] E. Stanley Jones, *In Christ* (Nashville, TN: Festival Books, Abingdon Press), 312.

I want to do with my life." In contrast, those who seek first Christ's kingdom say "no" to idleness and addiction.

As we age, it is too easy to succumb to nostalgia, resenting newer expressions of worship and renewal. Are you still passionate about God's future revivals? Many people involved in an earlier revival resist a newer revival because it doesn't look like the older revival. That is tragic.

Evangelist Bill Prankard, though he is a classic, old-school Pentecostal, has aged well. John Arnott invited Bill Prankard to speak at the Toronto Airport Fellowship's Catch the Fire meetings. Bill initially refused, saying that he was too old-school Pentecostal. John pushed back, saying "We need your healing anointing." Their friendship became a win-win. Prankard embodied those who say "no" to nostalgia and "yes" to the next revival.

Elijah said "yes" to the revival that God ultimately released on Elisha. Whom do you need to invest in that can be your Elisha?

A key verse that can help us finish well is *"...he who began a good work in you will carry it on to completion until the day of Christ Jesus"* (Philippians 1:6). We need to never settle down, never get stuck in a rut, never give up on life. E. Stanley Jones commented, "We don't grow old. We get older by not growing."[6]

Are you growing older gracefully? Are you still growing in creativity? As Christians, we grow from the inside out. God cares about producing true beauty of character. It is a good work that God has begun in us and will continue to carry out until he takes us home. There is no retirement from growing in Christ in the Christian life.

---

[6] E. Stanley Jones, *Growing Spiritually* (Nashville, TN: Abingdon Press, 1975), 350.

Winston Churchill, when he turned seventy-seven, commented, "We are happier in many ways when we grow old than when we were young. The young men sow wild oats. The old grow sage."[7]

In a study of four hundred outstanding people as reported by *Sunshine Magazine*,[8] researchers discovered that people in their sixties accomplish thirty-five percent of the world's greatest achievements, people in their seventies twenty-three percent, and people after age eighty produced eight percent. This means that sixty-four percent of the greatest achievements have been done by people aged sixty and over. Consider Michelangelo, who was writing poetry and designing buildings up to the time of his death at ninety.

Finishing well is about growing daily in gratitude. Elijah on Mount Horeb and John the Baptist in prison had lost sight of God's goodness in their lives. E. Stanley Jones wrote:

> To grow old, not only gracefully, but gratefully, is the Christian's privilege. For the Christian is not to bear old age but to use it. Is there any more utterly beautiful than a face, now grown old, but chiseled into tenderness and sympathy and experience?[9]

There is a beauty of holiness into which we can all grow in Christ. Think of Mother Teresa, as she poured out her life sacrificially for the least, the last, and the lost. Her gray hair truly was a crown of splendor (Proverbs 16:31).

Those who finish well live for others. Is life all about you and getting your way, or do others come first? Those who live

---

[7] E. Stanley Jones, *The Way* (Nashville, TN: Abingdon/Cokesbury Press, 1946), 283.

[8] Jones, *Growing Spiritually*, 310.

[9] Ibid., 313.

for others grow perpetually young in spirit. As Psalm 103:5 (NKJV) puts it, *"your youth is renewed like the eagle's."* And in Isaiah 40:31 (NKJV), we read, *"...those who wait on the LORD shall renew their strength, they shall mount up with wings like eagles."*

Secular retirement is often sold to people as getting something that they deserve. This is their time to focus on themselves first. E. Stanley Jones commented that:

> Those who come in "to enjoy themselves" the balance of their days wither prematurely and become inane and empty... Where there is no creative purpose, there is nothing but the creation of frustration.[10]

Every season of our lives has beautiful possibilities for fruitfulness. Think of Revelation 22:2, which describes the tree of life having unique fruit for each month. Whatever your age, do not fight the current season you are in. Embrace it and use it for God's glory. Your current season of life is full of adventure if you have eyes to see it.

May the Lord give us the courage and strength to bring forth lasting fruit even into our old age. With God's help, everyone can finish well.

> He shall be like a tree
>> Planted by the rivers of water,
>> That brings forth its fruit in its season,
>> Whose leaf also shall not wither;
>> And whatever he does shall prosper.
>> (Psalm 1:3, NKJV)

---

[10] Ibid., 312; Jones, *Mastery*, 350.

18

EVEN GREATER THINGS

Everyone was filled with awe
at the many wonders and signs
performed by the apostles.
(Acts 2:43)

On the evening before his trial and crucifixion, Jesus had what was surely one of his deepest and most intimate conversations with his disciples. What was on his mind as he shared these critical moments with his most dedicated followers?

Jesus spoke at length about the coming of the Holy Spirit, and the vital role the Spirit would play in the lives of the apostles and the early church. John devotes chapters fourteen to sixteen of his Gospel to this pivotal conversation. Early in that discussion Jesus makes this astonishing statement:

> Very truly I tell you, whoever believes in me will do the works I have been doing, and they will do even greater things than these, because I am going to the Father. (John 14:12)

How is this possible? Undoubtedly, the disciples were left speechless by that statement. They were eyewitnesses to the countless miracles Jesus had performed. How could they possibly do even greater works than their Lord?

Furthermore, this offer of miracle-working power was not and is not limited to the apostles. It is available widely—to whoever believes. There are no space or time limitations placed on Jesus' statement in John 14:12. The only limitation is our faith, since we know *"Jesus Christ is the same yesterday today and forever"* (Hebrews 13:8). Have we taken up the challenge our Lord laid out in John 14:12?

Jesus then goes on to say:

> And I will do whatever you ask in my name, so that the Father may be glorified in the Son. You may ask me for anything in my name, and I will do it. (John 14:13–14)

We confess that when we read this statement, we may feel like objecting, "Lord, don't you want to put some limitations on this amazing offer?"

Actually, there are some limitations built in. This amazing power and this ability is available *"so that the Father may be glorified in the Son."* In other words, ask for anything in my name but know this: All the glory, all the credit, all the fame belongs to Jesus.

Nothing limits the miracle-working power of God like the pride of the miracle-working agent. This is so because in truth the Holy Spirit is the miracle-working agent, not the human vessel. The glory must continually go to Jesus the Son.

Why could Jesus make this bold assertion that his followers would do greater things than he had?

First, Jesus knew the full power of the Holy Spirit. His entire ministry had been powered by the Holy Spirit. And the Father had revealed to him that in the coming days the same Holy Spirit would be poured out on his followers.

Secondly, Jesus knew the established biblical pattern. Holy Spirit power grows exponentially. Elijah came in the power of the Spirit. But his successor, Elisha, received a double portion of God's anointing. John the Baptist came in the power of the Spirit. But as John's successor, Jesus had access to a far greater power of the Spirit.

Unfortunately, Elisha's servant, Gehazi, due to his selfishness and greed, broke the chain of God's blessing. Had he not succumbed to sin, Gehazi may well have walked in a fourfold anointing. Humble, obedient faith is essential if we are going to walk in the full power of the Holy Spirit.

Jesus knew the exponentially-increasing power of the Holy Spirit would fall on his disciples. That is why Jesus could tell his followers that they would do greater things.

Did Jesus' word come true? It most certainly did. The phrase "signs and wonders" appears nine times in the book of Acts. We read that many people came to faith in Jesus Christ because of the signs and wonders that accompanied the preaching of the gospel. This is in addition to multiple miracles that are described in detail. The New Testament church was a miracle-working church where signs and wonders were common. This is why the first-century church experienced explosive growth across the Mediterranean world.

We need a return to Holy Spirit-powered church growth. How will that happen?

It begins with hunger—a hunger for the Holy Spirit, a hunger for Jesus to walk among us again. It begins with a hunger for God's word to be lived out among us.

In our earlier chapter on the Jesus movement, we pointed out that Acts 2:38 was the foundational verse for that revival. Acts 2:38 contains a threefold directive as spoken by the apostle Peter: *"Repent and be baptized, every one of you, in the name of Jesus Christ for the forgiveness of your sins. And you will receive the gift of the Holy Spirit."*

Simple obedience to that threefold directive brought spiritual life, healing, and restoration to millions. Underpinning the Jesus people revival was an Old Testament scripture drawn from Jeremiah 29.

But it was not the Jeremiah 29 scripture that is so frequently quoted today. Over the past twenty years, believers have zeroed in on Jeremiah 29:11. *"'For I know the plans I have for you,' declares the LORD, 'plans to prosper you and not to harm you, plans to give you hope and a future.'"*

The Old Testament focal point of the Jesus movement was the verses immediately after Jeremiah 29:11.

> "Then you will call on me and come and pray to me, and I will listen to you. You will seek me and find me when you seek me with all your heart. I will be found by you," declares the LORD, "and will bring you back from captivity. I will gather you from all the nations and places where I have banished you," declares the LORD, "and will bring you back to the place from which I carried you into exile." (Jeremiah 29:12–14)

The emphasis in that earlier revival was placed on seeking God. We will have hope and a future if we seek God. But without seeking, there is no finding. Without seeking God, we will remain lost and distant from him. The wonderful promise the LORD declares in Jeremiah 29:12–14 is, "I will be found by you."

The LORD will bring us back from our spiritual exile. This should be the cry of our hearts personally and corporately as the body of Christ. Many Jewish young people encountered their Messiah for the first time during the Jesus revolution of the early 1970s. For them, these verses from Jeremiah had a profound resonance.

This Old Testament passage has a New Testament counterpart drawn from Jesus' Sermon on the Mount: *"But seek first the kingdom of God and His righteousness, and all these things shall be added to you"* (Matthew 6:33, NKJV).

God meets with those who seek him. God is looking for hungry, seeking hearts. The Holy Spirit may find those hungry seeking hearts out in the world—or in your local church. Will we welcome the hungry hearts or turn them away because they do not meet our expectations or our standards?

Every revival has its own unique flavor and character. As a nineteen-year-old college student, David Kitz bore witness to a spontaneous outbreak of revival on campus. It was totally unexpected, uncontainable, and sustained for years. That experience set him on a quest to seek the Lord.

Let's prepare our hearts for what God is about to do. In this time of great spiritual darkness, God's promise remains.

> But to you who fear My name
>> The Sun of Righteousness shall arise
>> With healing in His wings… (Malachi 4:2, NKJV)

CONCLUSION

A code must be recognized, interpreted, and applied for it to be useful, and for it to effect meaningful change. Codes are recognized by the appearance of repetitive patterns. Through our examination of the lives and ministries of the Old Testament duo of Elijah and Elisha, and the New Testament duo of John the Baptist and Jesus, we can clearly see a pattern—a pattern of ever-increasing power and revelation.

In considerable detail, we have outlined how Elijah and John the Baptist are linked in terms of personality and the scope of their ministry. In the same way, we have detailed how the miracles and ministry of Jesus run parallel to the ministry of the prophet Elisha. The pattern is there for all to see.

What are the implications for Christians today? If we recognize this coded message in the Scriptures, how can it impact our lives in the twenty-first century?

Above all, *The Elisha Code* is a call to action. Yes, we can learn a great deal about the links between Elijah and John the Baptist and the links between Elisha and Jesus. But of first importance, we need the empowerment of the Holy Spirit to work within us and to transform our churches and society today.

The dynamic duos of this book were the greatest revivalists of their time. Elijah and Elisha brought about transformative change in Old Testament Israel. John the Baptist and Jesus set in motion the greatest spiritual transformation the world has ever seen—a transformation that continues to this day.

Here, then, are some key takeaways from studying the lives of these biblical dynamic duos and other revivalists and key figures in church history:

- Revivals/spiritual renewals have been an integral part of our faith from the time of ancient Israel to the present.
- When biblical truths are restored or reawakened, revival often follows.
- The age of miracles has not ended. We have Jesus' promise that believers will do even greater things (John 14:12).
- Genuine revivals are initiated by the Holy Spirit through fallible, imperfect human vessels (2 Timothy 2:20–22).
- Literary prophets have played, and will continue to play, an important role in fomenting revival and bringing about social and spiritual change.
- We need leaders with prophetic hindsight, insight, and foresight for the church to reach its full potential.
- Humility and selfless service are foundational in initiating and sustaining revival. The Spirit of God is quenched and grieved when pride, sin, or selfishness enter in (1 Thessalonians 5:19).
- Life-changing repentance is at the core of any authentic revival (Mark 1:15, Acts 2:38).
- The gospel message, according to Jesus, is all about regime change on a personal level. It's about letting King Jesus rule our hearts and minds (Colossians 1:13–14).
- True spiritual awakenings leap across religious, denominational, racial, and cultural barriers (Acts 10).

The most effective revivalists build bridges rather than walls.

- The church must remain focused on the core of the gospel message, rather than becoming swallowed by political agendas and yielding to the third temptation of Christ (Matthew 4:8–11).

- We are called to live a crucified life that elevates Christ and others by the power of relentless love and forgiveness (Galatians 2:20).

- God uses broken people who are yielded to his will (John 21:15–19).

- Hungry, humble prayer prepares a runway for the Holy Spirit to land, just as it did on the day of Pentecost (Acts 1:14, 2:1–4).

- Frequently, revivals begin where and when we least expect them, and they are often spearheaded by the young.

- Our goal should be to finish well. Our service to the Lord may involve many transitions, but his calling on our lives remains till we take our last breath (Romans 11:29).

Finally, the Elisha Code is a call to courageous and audacious faith.

Courage is a matter of the heart. The word "courage" is derived from the Latin word for heart. We must put our heart into our faith. Courageous faith flows from a heart that has been captured by the love of Jesus.

Let this be our prayer: Lord, give us courageous faith.

Audacious faith refuses to remain silent. It speaks out. It must speak.

After Elijah was swept up to heaven in a chariot of fire, Elisha did not remain silent. He spoke up with audacious faith.

Then he took the mantle of Elijah that had fallen from him, and struck the water, and said, "Where is the LORD God of Elijah?" And when he also had struck the water, it was divided this way and that; and Elisha crossed over. (2 Kings 2:14, NKJV)

Audacious faith is bold—bold like Elisha. The word "audacious" is derived from the same Latin root as "audio." Audacious faith makes noise. It must be heard. Is your faith loud enough to be heard by others? Is it being heard by God?

Jesus, whose New Testament miracles are patterned after Elisha's miracles, frequently chided his disciples for their lack of faith (Matthew 17:17–20).

Let this be our prayer: Lord Jesus, grant us a mustard seed of your courageous, audacious faith—mountain-moving faith. And as we walk our own Emmaus Road, light your fire in our hearts.

9 781486 624652